Village Prayer Bubbles

Daily Prayer Journal

by Vickie Henry

Cover photo and Vickie's photo
by Renee Steinpreis

ISBN 978-0-9982788-6-5

Scriptures used in book:

The Holy Bible, King James Version. Cambridge Edition: 1769;
King James Bible Online, 2019. www.kingjamesbibleonline.org.

Dedication

Village Prayer Bubbles is, first and foremost, dedicated to God. His presence is felt throughout Hot Springs Village. He shines through the trees, over the lakes and golf courses, and especially in the wonderful people who call HSV home. His hands guided the entire journal building process.

More than 24 churches in HSV exemplify God's love through His representatives here. We are God's family…people loving and caring for other people. We laugh together. We cry together. We pray together. I often envision one huge Sacred Bubble around the Village. Thank You, God, for this place we call home!

Next, this journal is dedicated to my greatest earthly blessing – my husband, Reb Henry. He has listened to me patiently as I relayed every incredible "God experience" that occurred as this journal came together. He would forgo his morning paper and coffee, giving his undivided attention when my friends' and contributing authors' stories spilled out of me excitedly. He has read and proofread for me, offering me his opinions and suggestions as I bounced ideas around. Reb is filled with the Holy Spirit and desires to serve our

Lord and does so in many wonderful ways…not the least, loving me as he loves the church, just as God commands. I thank God for him every day.

Finally, this book is dedicated to the 49 contributing authors. Not only did they write beautiful commentaries on their favorite verses, they did so prayerfully, as if doing it for the Lord Himself – which we did!

"Husbands, love your wives, just as Christ loved the church and gave himself up for her" Ephesians 5:25

"And we know that all things work together for good to them that love God, to them who are the called according to his purpose." Romans 8:28

"Whatever you do, work at it with all your heart, as working for the Lord, not for human masters," Colossians 3:23

Table of Contents

Introduction 7

Lessons:

1. A Healthy Move – Alice Hill 19
2. FOCUS on Vision – Jan Folstad 55
3. Servant Leadership – Warren Walters 89
4. Rock Bottom – Susan & Kara 125
5. The Blessings Bowl® – Linda Norman 159
6. My Journey in Song – Susan Rust 193
7. Planning for the Future – Becky Mueller 225
8. What if God Mystery Shopped YOU? 259
9. Forgiving the Unforgivable – Kathy Sanders 295
10. Angels Among Us – Steve Wilhite 327
11. The SCAT Family – Lynda Grasse 363
12. Bloom Where You Are Planted – Peggy Hadley 397

Afterward: Mini Bubbles of Faith 433

Contributing Authors 437

Acknowledgements 441

About the Author 443

A Note from Vickie 444

Introduction

Three years ago, when *Prayer Bubbles Daily Prayer Journal* was published, my prayer was, "Please, God, don't ask me to do this again."

The journal was a tremendous undertaking, born from the process of writing my book, *Prayer Bubbles.* Over the years, hardly a day has gone by without a phone call or email or text telling me how the journal has made a difference in someone's life. It has been one of my greatest blessings.

And then God asked me to do it again! After officially moving to Hot Springs Village two years ago, Reb and I found ourselves surrounded by the most incredible community of Christian neighbors: Pickleball players, golfers, parishioners, volunteers, card players, partiers, ping-pong advocates, and prayer warriors. We retirees have worked all of our lives and now spend lots of time playing and cherishing our new friendships.

So, a fresh group of faithful have joined together to create a new prayer journal entitled Village Prayer Bubbles Journal. All scripture verses have been chosen by residents of Hot Springs Village. Forty-nine contributing authors live in the Village.

How did Bubbles begin? Years ago, I realized that neither merely closing my eyes or kneeling would not help me focus as needed to speak with and listen to my Lord. In other words, my attention span was not what God deserved. After praying about my lack of prayer focus, God inspired a way for me to stay tuned in…written prayers. I first wrote my children's names at the top of my prayer page with a big circle around them. I prayed, "God, please put Whitney and Wade in Your Sacred Bubble, protect them, and bless them." The next circles contained my sisters, my nieces and nephews, friends, and soon, friends of friends. Prayer requests were included ("Will you put my mom in your Sacred Bubble? She just fell and broke her hip."). Before long, my morning journal pages were packed with names in bubbles. I had found God's calling for me – to provide prayer covering for people. I loved it!

In 2002, I wrote the poem God's Sacred Bubble.

"God's Sacred Bubble"

There is a place of solace,
A safe haven of love –
It's called God's Sacred Bubble
And He sends it from above.
Unlike this world of hurting,
Of scurrying to and fro,
Of watching loved ones fade away,

And feeling Oh-So-Low,
God's Bubble is protection
From the evil of this life.
It shields us from destruction,
From worry and from strife.
So, when you feel downtrodden
And your pain is crushing down,
Run to God's Sacred Bubble
Where His peace and grace are found.
And, as you pray for others
Your son, your mom, your friend,
Ask God to protect them
In His Bubble free from sin.
Oh, Thank You Lord for comfort,
For your sovereign security,
For Your Bubble that surrounds me
As I travel to Eternity.

God's Sacred Bubble was published in a couple of magazines and copies circulated among my friends and business associates. A good friend took the poem to her son who was in prison, and he made copies of it and gave it to fellow inmates. They began asking Mike about this God of his that accepted prayers in bubbles. Such joy to think this simple little poem might serve as bread crumbs leading someone to Christ.

Village Prayer Bubbles Journal is for everyone.

Though the writers happen to live in a little piece of the world called Arkansas, the scriptures and stories are intended for everyone everywhere.

Each contributing author has provided their name and contact information. Feel free to email them with any questions or comments. We welcome your feedback!

Please enjoy!

Vickie Henry
www. GodsSacredBubble.com
vickiehenry7@gmail.com

Make Bubbles

People ask me the "proper" way to use this journal: "Should I put one name in each bubble and pray for that person?" "Can I put more than one name in a bubble?" "Do I fill in every bubble?" "Can I add bubbles?"

Here is my answer: There are NO specific instructions. God does not put restrictions on us. They say it takes 21 days to develop a habit, good or bad, so begin journaling today and don't miss a day! When traveling, sometimes I copy 3-4 pages to avoid packing a big book. Make the journal your own – write as if no one but God will ever read it (this is probably the truth!). It's also okay to change your journaling style. You may write one name in a bubble on Monday and squeeze six into the same bubble on Tuesday.

In my journal, I scribble all over my daily page; however, others who journal have neat, pretty pages. This is wonderful, but hardly necessary. The truth is God is honored and glorified by all who seek Him. And we are the ones who receive the blessing. My early morning journaling time with the Lord sets the course for my entire day. With His armor (Ephesians 6) and my Prayer Bubbles circling me, I am peaceful and joyful.

First, I write the day and date at the top of the page. Now that I'm retired, doing so assists in keeping track of the current date. We didn't include a date on the journal pages so you may begin whenever you wish. God doesn't use the same calendar that we do.

Next, I read the scripture verse, take a deep breath of the Holy Spirit, and ponder the meaning, then move on to that day's message about that verse. Since most contributing authors are friends of mine, I feel blessed by their perspectives. Depending on your familiarity with the Village, I hope you enjoy this as well.

I reserve the big bubbles at the top for my children and grandchildren, and have a special small bubble for "Reb," my husband and my greatest earthly blessing. Tiny abbreviations are placed beside names: TM for traveling mercies when they are on trips, S for successful surgery, or P for someone who may be struggling spiritually, financially, physically, or in relationships. I know God recognizes my shorthand. With each bubble, I take time to pause and give God details about each person's special needs (as if He doesn't already know them. Ha!). Lastly, I like to text or email someone to let them know they have prayer covering.

When I began journaling, the 3 Things I am Thankful for Today were Faith, Health, and Peace. Now, I am very specific, giving thought to the previous day. An entry could include 1) Pickleball, 2) Lunch with Linda, and 3) My card from Warren.

For "What is the one thing God wants you to do for Him today?," I pray, then write the first thing that God puts on my heart. It could be call a friend or volunteer for AWL or clean my pantry. Sometimes, the thought God puts in my head is a complete surprise.

The only rule here is to journal. Spend that precious prayer time with God, while blessing your friends and family – even strangers – who need prayer covering and God's merciful hand on their lives.

* * *

Over nearly five decades, my prayer bubbles have been filled with special prayers for special people. Sometimes names have changed; some people are now with our Lord. Many names have had a space in my daily journal for years. The following are just a few of the people currently in my prayer bubbles.

Susan & Kara

While our Newcomer's class was learning to make a Chocolate Bark Roll, Susan received the news that her daughter, Kara, had been diagnosed with cancer. Susan had only been in the Village a few months, but had to rush back to Oklahoma to support her daughter.

They named the cancer Helga. Susan and Kara have faced this intrusion together, along with Kara's husband and 6-year-old son. Chemotherapy, radiation, and surgeries have ruled their lives for nearly a year now, which Kara has documented on her Facebook page *ChemowithKara.*

Susan wrote this to Kara:

> *"As your mother, I am so proud of the grace and perseverance you have shown as you face off with Helga. It amazes me how you have been able to turn such an ugly experience into a tool to help others fight their own "Helgas," and allow those around you to share in your journey. I will be with you every step of the way as God brings you through this. I have prayed specifically that Jesus is able to turn this experience into something that serves His purpose, and here you are doing just that as you witness through your blog."*

Kara recently posted this for her followers:

> *"God is saying to you today, I know you feel stressed and completely overwhelmed. But know this morning, I have your back. I am going to send you a blessing to remind you that I'm always in your corner. Don't give up. I am about to open some doors for you.*

These gals are heroes!

Melody

Steve

Betty

Three-year-old Melody is currently receiving chemotherapy. Our prayer is that the treatment is effective. Actually, our prayer is that the Great Physician will touch this precious child, heal her, and that her eye will be just fine, and she will grow to be a champion for Christ.

Whitney

My daughter, Whitney, is undergoing a series of tests to determine what is causing her to have problems swallowing. She discovered that she has high cholesterol, erratic blood pressure rates, and that her kidneys are not functioning properly. Whitney has been in a bubble for over 48 years and will continue to be for as long as I'm circling.

Wade

My son, Wade, and daughter-in-law, Melanie, have 4 of the most beautiful children that God ever put on this earth. I thank Him daily that they are healthy and happy and they have incredible parents. My prayer is for strength and discernment as Wade and Melanie raise these children to be champions for Him.

The ladies in then next bubbles have lost their husbands during the past year. Becky's story is detailed in Lesson 7: Planning for the Future. Phyllis is a contributing author and recently lost Joe, the love of her life. Nancy was married to Tony, both Pickleball players. In spite of pancreatic cancer, Tony kept playing on the courts until he couldn't. Pastor Dave Tappe went to the hospital with paddles and hit balls with Tony from his hospital bed. Rosie was in my Small Group Bible Study for years. She now lives in Mexico and lost her husband Ed earlier this year. She was in poor health even before Ed died, I do not know how she is faring now. She remains in God's Sacred Bubble every morning.

Becky
Phyllis
Nancy
Rosie

Johnny
& Linda

Johnny is an aerial firefighter and first responder. We pray for his safety daily. And his wife, Linda, is alone in the Village for several months while he is away. Both need our prayers.

With prayer bubbles, location, timeframe, or needs do not matter. Someone may be hurting financially, while another emotionally. God always cares. Many people are searching spiritually; they should be at the top of our prayer list. As much as we want people to be healthy and happy, we must always remember how brief this life is. We must do all we can to make sure our family and friends are spiritually healthy and happy. After all, we want to spend eternity with them.

God answers prayer, though it may not the answer we want from Him. Sometimes, the answer is no. Sometimes, He says go. And sometimes, the answer comes slowly. His timing may not be our timing. We must trust and obey…and continue to pray.

1. A Healthy Move

by Alice Hill

God sent many signs confirming that our move to Hot Springs Village was a good one. Jeremiah 29:11 assured me that He had plans to prosper me and not harm me, to give me hope for the future. After living in my one and only hometown, my husband had found this "jewel of a place" and convinced me that retiring and moving there was a grand idea. It would be an adventure! So, why was moving so hard? Why was I downtrodden?

The excitement of relocating to a new home, furnishing it, and finding our way around a new area got me through the first few weeks. Everyone we met was so friendly; it felt like Utopia. But there was uneasiness deep in my soul…a desperate need for connections, for purpose, for feeling significant. Time spent with my Lord became very necessary and especially precious, providing the familiar and solid ground in my new home. Trusting the Lord with all my heart became monumental.

One Sunday, while welcoming me at Village Bible Church, a lady named Ana placed a little yellow postcard in my palm – an invitation to join A Healthy Move. Was this a fitness class? Actually, the answer was yes, and a bit more. A Healthy Move charted my course to be spiritually, physically, emotionally, and socially healthy.

Ruth Neal developed the criteria for A Healthy Move. As a trusting believer, she had taken her own transitional challenges to the Lord, then studied, listened with a learner's heart, and wrote down what He was teaching her. Ruth's efforts helped guide what began as a friendship class into a 12-lesson curriculum covering the very concerns she had experienced.

Each lesson had a scriptural foundation, with welcome opportunities to learn about each other and our community. I discovered other women who were struggling with the same rollercoaster of emotions that comes from being uprooted from family, friends, and all things familiar. We had been transplanted, and our new roots were shallow and shaky.

Friendships developed immediately. A feeling of community surrounded me throughout those weeks. I began to recognize and chat with friends while shopping at Wal-Mart! Bonds were built as we lunched together and learned more about each other. Camaraderie grew as we traveled together on field trips or to local places of interest.

Two things every person needs: 1) to feel valued and 2) to feel like they belong. A Healthy Move provided both for all who participated. Together, we shared strategies to weather the ups and downs of life, while encouraging one another to keep our eyes on Jesus. Many call A Healthy Move their "lifeline;" others say that's where they met their best friend.

Needless to say, these strangers became like family. We have created lasting friendships while socializing and attending Bible studies together through the years. We became a living example of the logo for our class… women walking side by side toward a cross.

"Let us then approach God's throne of grace with confidence, so that we may receive mercy and find grace to help us in our time of need." Hebrews 4:16

My Mother's Novena

When our family had a great need for God's help, my mother would make a 9-hour novena including this passage. It was a wonderful petition to Him. When I had my own family, we carried on the tradition by saying the novena prayer whenever we took a road trip. Each hour we would petition God for safe travels.

~Dotti K.

"'Ask and it will be given to you; seek and you will find; knock and the door will be opened to you.'"

Matthew 7:7

3 things I am thankful for today:

1.__________

2.__________

3.__________

What is one thing God wants me to do for Him today?

God's Way is not the World's Way

"Then he said to them all: 'Whoever wants to be my disciple must deny themselves and take up their cross daily and follow me.'"

Luke 9:23

What did Jesus mean by, "Take up their cross daily?" Have you known someone with strength and peace during hardships? I knew a family whose 2-year-old drowned. At his graveside, they sang him a lullaby, just as they did every night. In my eyes, they had taken up their cross.

~Phillis R.

3 things I am thankful for today:

1.________________________

2.________________________

3.________________________

What is one thing God wants me to do for Him today?

Perseverence

Trials act as refining tools in life. They cause change in behavior and attitude and help us to rely more on God. When we persevere despite personal hardship, God speaks to our heart by His Word and helps us to see things from His perspective. Testing and trials yield spiritual maturity.

~Chris C.

"Blessed is the one who perseveres under trial because, having stood the test, that person will receive the crown of life that the Lord has promised to those who love him."

James 1:12

3 things I am thankful for today:

1.____________________

2.____________________

3.____________________

What is one thing God wants me to do for Him today?

Taking Care of God's Temple

"Don't you know that you yourselves are God's temple and that God's Spirit dwells in your midst?"
1 Corinthians 3:16

When I think about my body as God's temple, I recall the importance of taking good care of it physically, as well as spiritually. Yes, I should eat healthy food, exercise regularly, and get adequate rest, but I should also take care of this temple through spiritual disciplines such as prayer, Bible study, and corporate worship.

~Debbie R.

3 things I am thankful for today:

1.____________________

2.____________________

3.____________________

What is one thing God wants me to do for Him today?

Think About Such Things

We are bombarded by frightening news images and unsavory entertainment. How do we control what gets free rent in our heads? Halt bad memories by saying, "Stop! Jesus and I survived that!" and dismissing unwanted thoughts with praise like, "Thank You, Jesus".

~Sharon B.

"Finally, brothers and sisters, whatever is true, whatever is noble, whatever is right, whatever is pure, whatever is lovely, whatever is admirable—if anything is excellent or praiseworthy—think about such things."

Philippians 4:8

3 things I am thankful for today:

1.____________________

2.____________________

3.____________________

What is one thing God wants me to do for Him today?

Study

"Study to shew thyself approved unto God, a workman that needeth not to be ashamed, rightly dividing the word of truth."

2 Timothy 2:15 (KJV)

While studying God's word is not necessary to get to Heaven, we should study the Bible. One of the most enjoyable things I do is study, not just read, the Bible. Webster's 1828 Dictionary, a Greek/Hebrew Concordance, and cross-referencing verses can be tremendous help in fully understanding the Bible.

~Steve R.

3 things I am thankful for today:

1.____________________

2.____________________

3.____________________

What is one thing God wants me to do for Him today?

Purchased By Jesus' Blood

Having been saved by the blood of the Lamb, Jesus, I look forward to going to heaven and meeting people from every nation who were also purchased by Jesus. It will be an awesome sight.

~Julie K

"And they sang a new song, saying: 'You are worthy to take the scroll and to open its seals, because you were slain, and with your blood you purchased for God persons from every tribe and language and people and nation.'"

Revelation 5:9

3 things I am thankful for today:

1.__________

2.__________

3.__________

What is one thing God wants me to do for Him today?

Future in the Rear View Mirror

"For I know the plans I have for you," declares the Lord, "plans to prosper you and not to harm you, plans to give you hope and a future. Then you will call on me and come and pray to me, and I will listen to you."

Jeremiah 29:11-12

Sometimes, the only way you become aware of His plans is through the 20/20 hindsight! Had God unfolded His 20-year plan for me years ago, doubtless it would have been too daunting to contemplate; I probably would have "chickened" out! What a life I'd have missed out on!

~Warren W.

3 things I am thankful for today:

1.____________________

2.____________________

3.____________________

What is one thing God wants me to do for Him today?

imPOSSIBLE

Sometimes, I try and solve issues myself, but on occasion, I forget that, without God, we can do nothing. We need to step back, let go, and let God take control. His will is what we want. Let Him show up and show out, for He has all of the power and control.

~Donna P.

"Jesus looked at them and said, 'With man this is impossible, but with God all things are possible.'"
Matthew 19:26

3 things I am thankful for today:

1.__________

2.__________

3.__________

What is one thing God wants me to do for Him today?

Security

"Whoever dwells in the shelter of the Most High will rest in the shadow of the Almighty."

Psalm 91:1

Hot Springs Village can be a place of safety and refuge. Village first-responders, police, firefighters, EMT's and SCAT volunteers provide for our physical well-being, but each of us must seek our own spiritual refuge.

~Patty M.

3 things I am thankful for today:

1.____________________

2.____________________

3.____________________

What is one thing God wants me to do for Him today?

A Gift for Everyone

God, has handed you a gift: His Son, Jesus. Decision time! Will you reject Jesus, leaving Him in the gift-box, not wanting His involvement in your life? Or will you receive Jesus into your daily life to be your friend and guiding light-of-truth throughout your earthly life, then joyfully living together for eternity in Heaven?

~Ruth N.

"For God so loved the world that he gave his one and only Son, that whoever believes in him shall not perish but have eternal life."

John 3:16

3 things I am thankful for today:

1.________________

2.________________

3.________________

What is one thing God wants me to do for Him today?

It's Not Just Heart

"Do not conform to the pattern of this world, but be transformed by the renewing of your mind. Then you will be able to test and approve what God's will is—his good, pleasing and perfect will."
Romans 12:2

Being transformed by Christ requires changing our thought processes as well as our heart. Thinking is really about the questions we ask ourselves, our self-talk. How much intellectual work do I put into changing my thoughts and thinking differently?

~Jim H.

____

____

____

____

____

____

____

____

____

____

____

____

____

____

____

____

____

3 things I am thankful for today:

1.____________________________

2.____________________________

3.____________________________

What is one thing God wants me to do for Him today?

____

Faith – Praying for My Prodi-

I believe God is who He says He is, The Almighty God. Therefore, with confident faith, I courageously stand in the dark moments. Standing, waiting, not knowing all the answers nor the timing of God's answer. Waiting, not in frustration or anger or fear, but with calm patience because I know I can trust God.

~Debi S.

"I remain confident of this: I will see the goodness of the Lord in the land of the living. Wait for the Lord; be strong and take heart and wait for the Lord."

Psalm 27: 13-14

3 things I am thankful for today:

1.__________

2.__________

3.__________

What is one thing God wants me to do for Him today?

Luv Buds

"Greater love has no one than this: to lay down one's life for one's friends."

John 15:13

John 15:13 reminds me of the song "I'd Do Anything For You" from the musical *Oliver*. We all have found dear friends that are soul-mates, and I venture to say we would go to the "nth" degree for them. This is because they share our core values and spiritual beliefs, not just our hobbies and favorite foods.

~LunaGram

3 things I am thankful for today:

1.____________________

2.____________________

3.____________________

What is one thing God wants me to do for Him today?

Sickness? Don't Give Up

Sickness doesn't have to keep us down. While enduring treatment for leukemia, I know that I could let this disease get the best of me, but I have a God who is stronger and more powerful that any disease. Yes, Lord, I will pick up my mat and walk with You. Lord, walk with me.

~Phillis R.

"Then Jesus said to him, 'Get up! Pick up your mat and walk.'"

John 5:8

3 things I am thankful for today:

1.________________

2.________________

3.________________

What is one thing God wants me to do for Him today?

Blind Spots

"You hypocrite, first take the plank out of your own eye, and then you will see clearly to remove the speck from your brother's eye."

Matthew 7:5

We are quick to point out others' faults, sometimes to the point that we deny forgiveness. Often, we are blinded by our pride, which hides our own flaws from us. When we humble ourselves by recognizing our flaws, forgiveness is easier.

~Ike E.

3 things I am thankful for today:

1.____________________

2.____________________

3.____________________

What is one thing God wants me to do for Him today?

Ask for Peace

I once received a scam letter, which I threw in the trash. Then curiosity won, so I called. They asked for my Social Security number, and I gave it! I knew I had done a stupid thing and prayed for God's forgiveness. He forgave, but I could not forgive myself. I felt heavy; so I asked for God's peace. Suddenly, I felt like I had wings to fly! Praise God!

~Bess M.

"Do not be anxious about anything, but in every situation, by prayer and petition, with thanksgiving, present your requests to God. And the peace of God, which transcends all understanding, will guard your hearts and your minds in Christ Jesus."

Philippians 4:6-7

3 things I am thankful for today:

1.__________

2.__________

3.__________

What is one thing God wants me to do for Him today?

We Can Have Victory!

"Casting down imaginations, and every high thing that exalteth itself against the knowledge of God, and bringing into captivity every thought to the obedience of Christ;"

2 Corinthians 10:5 (KJV)

How often do we say, "I can't help it," when our minds are flooded with overwhelming thoughts? God says we CAN help it! Through Him and the Word, we can bring every thought into captivity. Rebuke those worrisome thoughts in Jesus' name! By His power, we can be victorious over our thoughts!

~Suzan R.

3 things I am thankful for today:

1.____________________

2.____________________

3.____________________

What is one thing God wants me to do for Him today?

Where Were You?

This is possibly the most humbling verse in the Bible. And just like Job, we tend to question God. Why am I ill? Why did my husband die? Our Sovereign God is our Creator. We will never understand His ways, but He calls us to have faith. Cling to His promises; His plan is perfect.

~Vickie H.

"'Where were you when I laid the earth's foundation? Tell me, if you understand.'"

Job 38:4

3 things I am thankful for today:

1.__________

2.__________

3.__________

What is one thing God wants me to do for Him today?

Do Know Where You Are Going?

"Trust in the Lord with all your heart and lean not on your own understanding; in all your ways submit to him, and he will make your paths straight."
Proverbs 3:5-6

Driving in Arkansas, I often get lost. When I enter the address in my GPS, the drive is less stressful. Living life is like that. Trying to do it on my own is a mess. When I trust God to direct my path, especially when I do not know the way, He does. He IS the way.

~Teela Y.

3 things I am thankful for today:

1.____________________

2.____________________

3.____________________

What is one thing God wants me to do for Him today?

The Faucet of Faith

While reading research about children and success in school, I found this definition: Being poor means you have no money. Being in poverty means you have no hope. Is your soul living in poverty? As you trust the Lord, you will find not only overflowing hope, but joy and peace. Give your hopelessness over to Him.

~Diane G.

"May the God of hope fill you with all joy and peace as you trust in him, so that you may overflow with hope by the power of the Holy Spirit."
Romans 15:13

3 things I am thankful for today:

1.__________

2.__________

3.__________

What is one thing God wants me to do for Him today?

Mending Broken Hearts

"The Lord is close to the brokenhearted and saves those who are crushed in spirit."

Psalm 34:18

We all have had broken hearts. Life disappoints us, our friends desert us, and God can seem far away. Take heart – God promises He will never leave us. So be still and allow His Holy Spirit to fill you up, to refresh you as only God can do.

~Debbie R.

3 things I am thankful for today:

1.________________________

2.________________________

3.________________________

What is one thing God wants me to do for Him today?

Be a Doer, Not Just a Hearer

How do we know what God is asking us to do? We often don't hear God because most of us are better at talking than listening. We must ask God, then be quiet and listen for His answer. God has planted us in a particular place and told us to be the best we possibly can be at whatever He has called us to do.

~Steve B.

"Do not merely listen to the word, and so deceive yourselves. Do what is says."

James 1:22

3 things I am thankful for today:

1.____________________

2.____________________

3.____________________

What is one thing God wants me to do for Him today?

Am I Wobbly?

"And Jesus grew in wisdom and stature, and in favor with God and man."

Luke 2:52

Jesus grew intellectually, physically, spiritually, and socially. Imagine a stool with four legs: each leg is important and offers stability. If not balanced, the stool wobbles. As Christians, we are to be imitators of Christ. Are you stable or wobbly? Grow as He grew!

~Betty W.

3 things I am thankful for today:

1.____________________

2.____________________

3.____________________

What is one thing God wants me to do for Him today?

Hemmed In

God has His hands all over my life, from beginning to end. I am safe in those hands. He has stitched up my life in a tapestry of His making and He is doing divine things. My past, my future, all are in His hands. No matter that I can't always see what He's doing. He has a plan, and that is enough.

~Marilyn C.

"You hem me in behind and before, and you lay your hand upon me. Such knowledge is too wonderful for me, too lofty for me to attain."

Psalm 139:5-6

3 things I am thankful for today:

1.____________________

2.____________________

3.____________________

What is one thing God wants me to do for Him today?

But Be Very Careful

"...But be very careful to keep the commandment...that Moses...gave you: to love the Lord your God, to walk in obedience to him, to keep his commands, to hold fast to him and to serve him with all your heart and with all your soul."

Joshua 22:4-5

When God grants our requests, don't become cavalier in spiritual thoughts and actions. When all goes well is the time to evaluate our commitment to Bible study, prayer, and vigilance in following God's commandments. "Be very careful," for our enemy is watching, and will place his trap near slipping spiritual feet.

~Ruth N.

3 things I am thankful for today:

1.________________________

2.________________________

3.________________________

What is one thing God wants me to do for Him today?

Be Ready

A wise Arkansas grandmother advised her children and grandchildren to "Stay prayed up!" Sound advice! No one knows when Jesus will return nor when our personal passage to eternal life will come. Lord, thank You for the opportunity to pray without ceasing, confident You'll fill our needs in this life and the next.

~Chris S.

"It will be good for those servants whose master finds them watching when he comes…"

Luke 12:37

3 things I am thankful for today:

1.____________________

2.____________________

3.____________________

What is one thing God wants me to do for Him today?

First, Count to Three

"Finally, brothers and sisters, whatever is true, whatever is noble, whatever is right, whatever is pure, whatever is lovely, whatever is admirable–if anything is excellent or praiseworthy–think about such things."

Philippians 4:8

Words and the way we say them are so powerful. We can crush a spirit with quick, critical words. Likewise, gentle, encouraging words can build up a spirit. A good practice is to count to three (Father, Son, Holy Spirit) before we speak, so that our words will be remembered positively. Today, pray for God's help in speaking positive words into the world.

~Sharon B.

3 things I am thankful for today:

1.____________________

2.____________________

3.____________________

What is one thing God wants me to do for Him today?

Even When We Doubt

How often I take a tentative step or two in faith, only to allow doubt to creep in. Will God really give me the strength to live victoriously? YES! And while gently chiding me for doubting Him, He is stretching out His hand to catch me in my unbelief.

~Kathy C.

"'Come,' he said. Then Peter got down out of the boat, walked on the water and came toward Jesus. But when he saw the wind, he was afraid and, beginning to sink, cried out, 'Lord, save me!' Immediately Jesus reached out his hand and caught him. 'You of little faith,' he said, 'why did you doubt?'"

Matthew 14:29-31

3 things I am thankful for today:

1.____________________

2.____________________

3.____________________

What is one thing God wants me to do for Him today?

Wonder Woman

"Charm is deceptive,
and beauty is fleeting;
but a woman who
fears the Lord
is to be praised."

Proverbs 31:30

Yes, a worthy wife's worth is far beyond pearls, but I don't know any woman alive or dead who could live up to the description of an "ideal" wife in this proverb. We'd like to be talented, wise, strong, generous, creative and loving, but often spend too much time on beauty and charm. It's better to focus on the Lord.

~Paula D.

3 things I am thankful for today:

1.________________________

2.________________________

3.________________________

What is one thing God wants me to do for Him today?

What Is Your Plan?

Struggling with the decision to move to Hot Springs Village. I prayed, "Will I be happy here? Should I leave my grandchildren in Dallas? I'll miss my old friends!" My friend Sharon enlightened me, saying, "Vickie, God has a purpose for you in Arkansas!" This gave me a whole new perspective! My prayers changed from "Will 'I'?" to "What is Your plan, Lord?"

~Vickie H.

"And we know that in all things God works for the good of those who love him, who have been called according to his purpose."

Romans 8:28

3 things I am thankful for today:

1.__________

2.__________

3.__________

What is one thing God wants me to do for Him today?

2. FOCUS on Vision

by Jan Folstad, Founder

"I would rather walk with a friend in the dark, than alone in the light. The best and most beautiful things in the world cannot be seen or even touched. They must be felt with the heart. Death is no more than passing from one room into another. But there's a difference for me, you know. Because in that other room I shall be able to see." ~Helen Keller

It is a bright sunny day in Hot Springs Village. Imagine that you have just returned from your annual eye exam. The doctor's news was not bright or sunny. "You have the beginning of macular degeneration." What does this mean for your future? Fear grips you. You need a friend.

Enter the FOCUS Program. FOCUS is a program for Villagers experiencing low vision. We have a high percentage of AMD (age-related macular degeneration), but also deal with glaucoma, diabetic retinopathy, and other various eye diseases – anyone with limited vision.

Jan Folstad heads up a totally volunteer group of 12 or so staff/teachers with big hearts, strong faith, and a compassionate desire to help. Our motto is, "We step in where your eye doctor leaves off." For over 20 years, our program has been a blessing to Villagers by teaching alternative ways to do daily tasks, thereby helping them to remain safe and independent.

- How do you tell your navy blue slacks from your black slacks?
- How do you mark or identify your medications?
- How do you measure flour for your family's favorite Christmas cookies?
- When do you decide to give up driving?

Monthly support groups and formal in-depth annual classes help to answer these questions. For example, lighting and contrast are important, but light needs very from person to person. We explore different types of magnification and what works best for each individual. Another strategy is to mark kitchen utensils, clothing, and cosmetics with dots made from Puffy Paint, an inexpensive paint that adheres to just about everything and stays on forever. We're pretty creative!

In our cooking class, we get all students involved in the kitchen. One gentleman cracked his first egg EVER! He was so excited that he called his children that evening to tell them about it.

Many friendships have been formed during our classes. For instance, our students receive a special pair of sunglasses which do not fit into any cases found at the store. To remedy this, we have a class where students make their own out of potholders. We have a wonderful photo of two older gentlemen who became friends in class sitting together and enjoying each other's company while sewing their glasses cases.

A sentiment often expressed by our students is learning they are not alone in their journey with vision loss. Denial is prevalent. One very reluctant student explained that she was so busy she probably wouldn't attend all of the classes. After her first class, she cancelled all other commitments and showed up for every class. By replacing reluctance and resistance with anticipation and appreciation, she became one of our strongest advocates.

Thank God for FOCUS!

> *"Now faith is confidence in what we hope for and assurance about what we do not see."* Hebrews 11:1

You Can Be Sure!

God wants His kids to know where they stand with Him. If you are a believer in Jesus, He says you have eternal life. He wants you to know that you are His – not to question or to hope or to guess, but to KNOW. He gives us that assurance in His word.

~Marilyn C.

"I write these things to you who believe in the name of the Son of God so that you may know that you have eternal life. This is the confidence we have in approaching God: that if we ask anything according to his will, he hears us. And if we know that he hears us–whatever we ask–we know that we have what we asked of him."

1 John 5:13-15

3 things I am thankful for today:

1.__________

2.__________

3.__________

What is one thing God wants me to do for Him today?

Without It, We Have Nothing

"Keep me safe, my God, for in you I take refuge."
Psalm 16:1

"Trust God to do what you cannot. Obey God, and do what you can." (credit Max Lucado) That five-letter word is the essence. Without trust, we have nothing. If you can't trust your marriage partner, your business partner, your kids, friends, family or yourself, then there is no foundation!

~Warren W.

3 things I am thankful for today:

1.____________________

2.____________________

3.____________________

What is one thing God wants me to do for Him today?

Hearing That Little Voice

Before I was even born, God wrote His law on my heart. That little voice that convicts me when my thoughts are not pure. My conscience tells me the action I'm considering would displease Him. I'm so thankful God's moral law resides in me. With each day I strive to heed it to please Him.

~Debbie R.

"I desire to do your will, my God; your law is within my heart."

Psalm 40:8

3 things I am thankful for today:

1.__________

2.__________

3.__________

What is one thing God wants me to do for Him today?

Even If No One Is Looking

"'Whoever can be trusted with very little can also be trusted with much, and whoever is dishonest with very little will also be dishonest with much.'"

Luke 16:10

Honesty and integrity define character. Cheating is cheating, whether it's accepting $1 too much in change or embezzling a million dollars. Catching someone in dishonest conduct causes us to doubt everything we know about them. As Christians, we need to be honest to our cores, not giving others a reason to doubt us or to stumble themselves.

~Sharon B.

3 things I am thankful for today:

1.____________________________

2.____________________________

3.____________________________

What is one thing God wants me to do for Him today?

Pray, Don't Worry

Years ago, I cross-stitched a poem for my mother-in-law, which I still recite to myself when I start to feel concerned: "If a care is too small to be turned into a prayer, it is too small to be made into a burden." So, pray; don't worry.

~Reba L.

"'Therefore I tell you, do not worry about your life, what you will eat or drink; or about your body, what you will wear. Is not life more than food, and the body more than clothes?'"

Matthew 6:25

3 things I am thankful for today:

1.____________________

2.____________________

3.____________________

What is one thing God wants me to do for Him today?

We Serve an Amazing God

"'For the Lord your God is the one who goes with you to fight for you against your enemies to give you victory.'"

Deuteronomy 20:4

No one likes war. A battlefield is hard to look at, much less live in. But we are in a war – living in a spiritual battlefield. The good news is our Lord is here, fighting in the filth right beside us, being our protector. The battle is dark and painful at times, but keep fighting with Him. God's victory is near!

~Ruth N.

3 things I am thankful for today:

1.________________

2.________________

3.________________

What is one thing God wants me to do for Him today?

The Spirit Within

God knows that we need help to achieve His plan. We each have the Holy Spirit within us to teach us, comfort us, and help us along. If we listen to the Spirit and follow what He tells us to do, we will have the blessings that God plans for us.

~Tanya J.

"But the Advocate, the Holy Spirit, whom the Father will send in my name, will teach you all things and will remind you of everything I have said to you."

John 14:26

3 things I am thankful for today:

1.________________

2.________________

3.________________

What is one thing God wants me to do for Him today?

Always Obey

"And the Lord God commanded the man, 'You are free to eat from any tree in the garden; but you must not eat from the tree of the knowledge of good and evil, for when you eat from it you will certainly die.'"

Genesis 2:16-17

Adam and Eve understood God's command and chose to disobey Him. They did not understand the consequences of their sin , but God knew. If He says no or to wait, we should obey because He knows a lot more than we do. He could be saving us from pain or working on a wonderful blessing for us to enjoy.

~Donna P.

3 things I am thankful for today:

1.____________________

2.____________________

3.____________________

What is one thing God wants me to do for Him today?

It's Okay to be Silent

Sometimes you just can't win. Sometimes it seems nothing you say will change anything. Even when you're nervous and afraid, people will think you're ignorant, but you won't convince them by talking needlessly. It's okay to be silent.

~Jim H.

"When he was accused by the chief priests and the elders, he gave no answer. Then Pilate asked him, 'Don't you hear the testimony they are bringing against you?' But Jesus made no reply, not even to a single charge– to the great amazement of the governor."

Matthew 27:12-14

3 things I am thankful for today:

1.________________

2.________________

3.________________

What is one thing God wants me to do for Him today?

As Christ Forgave You

"Bear with each other and forgive one another if any of you has a grievance against someone. Forgive as the Lord forgave you."
Colossians 3:13

We have the best example, Jesus Christ. Yet, forgiving others is often so very difficult for us! Christ forgave without even being asked, without even hearing the word "sorry." Instead, even when he was arrested, put on trial, beaten, and crucified, He forgave!! Furthermore, He instructed us to do likewise!

~Vickie H.

3 things I am thankful for today:

1.____________________

2.____________________

3.____________________

What is one thing God wants me to do for Him today?

Conform Versus Transform

Each morning, we draw close to God in our devotional time and read His Word, trying to understand what He might be saying to us. May we ask Him to help us focus on the important things for that day by quieting our spirit and helping us to prioritize. At day's end, we will see where God transformed and orchestrated our day.

~Chris C.

"Do not conform to the pattern of this world, but be transformed by the renewing of your mind. Then you will be able to test and approve what God's will is–his good, pleasing and perfect will."
Romans 12:2

3 things I am thankful for today:

1.________

2.________

3.________

What is one thing God wants me to do for Him today?

Tithing

"Be sure to set aside a tenth of all that your fields produce each year."

Deuteronomy 14:22

When we write that tithe check each week, we do it as an act of faith. We are saying, "God, we are returning to You one-tenth of what is already Yours and we trust You to provide for us. We promise to be good stewards with the rest." When we do this faithfully, God never lets us down.

~Steve B.

3 things I am thankful for today:

1.____________________

2.____________________

3.____________________

What is one thing God wants me to do for Him today?

Temptation?

This is the second verse I ever memorized. Over the years, God has proven His faithfulness by showing me ways to escape temptation. Sometimes a simple interruption causes me to change direction. Sometimes a "check" will enter my mind, or a "yeah, but..." will cause me to bite my tongue. How I thank God for His faithfulness.

~Sue K.

"No temptation has overtaken you except what is common to mankind. And God is faithful; he will not let you be tempted beyond what you can bear. But when you are tempted, he will also provide a way out so that you can endure it."

1 Corinthians 10:13

3 things I am thankful for today:

1.________________

2.________________

3.________________

What is one thing God wants me to do for Him today?

Lost Child

"'For this is what the Sovereign Lord says: I myself will search for my sheep and look after them.'"

Ezekiel 34:11

If you have ever lost sight of your child, perhaps at a store, an amusement park, or just in your own home, it's scary! But God always has His eyes on them. Do you have a lost child now? Take heart and continue to pray for them, for their Father in Heaven knows exactly where they are.

~Becky M.

3 things I am thankful for today:

1.____________________

2.____________________

3.____________________

What is one thing God wants me to do for Him today?

How to Heal Our Land

This passage is quite clear: what will bring healing to our land is God's people getting right. We spend a lot of time fretting over the actions of non-Christian people, fearing that God is judging this nation because of them. However, God is judging this nation because His people are not doing the things outlined in His word.

~Suzan R.

"If my people, which are called by my name, shall humble themselves, and pray, and seek my face, and turn from their wicked ways; then will I hear from heaven, and will forgive their sin, and will heal their land."

2 Chronicles 7:14 (KJV)

3 things I am thankful for today:

1.____________________

2.____________________

3.____________________

What is one thing God wants me to do for Him today?

Remove the Weight!

"Then I acknowledged my sin to you and did not cover up my iniquity. I said, 'I will confess my transgressions to the Lord.' And you forgave the guilt of my sin."

Psalm 32:5

Confessing our sins can be very difficult. Sometimes we try to cover them up or ignore them, hoping they go away. But their weight remains on our shoulders until we confess them to God. He forgives us, remembers our sins no more, and the weight is removed. Praise be to God!

~Debbie R.

3 things I am thankful for today:

1.____________________

2.____________________

3.____________________

What is one thing God wants me to do for Him today?

He is Here

Blessedly, our loving Father didn't leave us orphans after the Passion and Resurrection. We are given Jesus' true presence in the Eucharist, and He breathed the Holy Spirit upon the disciples. We, too, are gifted with the Advocate to intercede for us to the Father and Son. Amazing grace, may we remain thankful we are never alone!

~Chris S.

"and teaching them to obey everything I have commanded you. And surely I am with you always, to the very end of the age.'"

Matthew 28:20

3 things I am thankful for today:

1.__________

2.__________

3.__________

What is one thing God wants me to do for Him today?

You Are Protected

"But the Lord is faithful, and he will strengthen you and protect you from the evil one."

2 Thessalonians 3:3

I pray the Prayer to St. Michael often these days! There is so much evil and ugliness in this world. I must admit I don't always have the confidence that I am protected, and shame on me! I ask that you would pray for me to have more trust in the good Lord to ease my fears and help me through the spiritual life as well!

~LunaGram

3 things I am thankful for today:

1.____________________

2.____________________

3.____________________

What is one thing God wants me to do for Him today?

Take Control

Verse 5 states that, through our weapons of warfare, we can control our thoughts, life, and everything in our life that would try to exalt itself above God. Our weapons of warfare are (Ephesians 6): always be truthful, live right, share the gospel with others, trust God, be assured of your salvation, and know God's word.

~Steve R.

"Casting down imaginations, and every high thing that exalteth itself against the knowledge of God, and bringing into captivity every thought to the obedience of Christ;"

2 Corinthians 10:5 (KJV)

3 things I am thankful for today:

1.____________________

2.____________________

3.____________________

What is one thing God wants me to do for Him today?

We are Called to Obey

"Therefore, my dear friends, as you have always obeyed—not only in my presence, but now much more in my absence—continue to work out your salvation with fear and trembling, for it is God who works in you to will and to act in order to fulfill his good purpose."
Philippians 2:12-13

God did not just save us from something; He saved us for something. That is to participate actively in service to others as we follow the spiritual journey He has laid out for us.

~Jody M.

3 things I am thankful for today:

1.____________________

2.____________________

3.____________________

What is one thing God wants me to do for Him today?

Values

In this time of testing, I remember a wise old comic strip "POGO," whose main character said, "I have seen the enemy, and he is us." As civility and morality in living and governing are being challenged at every turn, we must focus on the truth of God's holy words.

~Patty M.

"The Lord is my light and my salvation–whom shall I fear? The Lord is the stronghold of my life–of whom shall I be afraid?"

Psalm 27:1

3 things I am thankful for today:

1.____________________

2.____________________

3.____________________

What is one thing God wants me to do for Him today?

Choosing the Better Part

"'Martha, Martha,' the Lord answered, 'you are worried and upset about many things, but few things are needed—or indeed only one. Mary has chosen what is better, and it will not be taken away from her.'"

Luke 10:41-42

We are so blessed in HSV with opportunities to serve our neighbors and friends, especially the needy and poor. Yet, we can easily be so caught up in activities that busy-ness can actually hinder our spiritual life. Here, Jesus reminds me that the most important thing is to be still and listen to the voice of God in the silence of my heart and prayer.

~Paula D.

3 things I am thankful for today:

1.____________________

2.____________________

3.____________________

What is one thing God wants me to do for Him today?

GPS: God's Purpose Server

Remember how proud we were when our children made good grades? Don't you know we please God when we spend time studying His Word and use it as a GPS as we travel through our day? The world can twist our thinking, making it easy to justify wrongdoing. The Bible brings us back to the truth!

~Vickie H.

"Do your best to present yourself to God as one approved, a worker who does not need to be ashamed and who correctly handles the word of truth."

2 Timothy 2:15

____

____

____

____

____

____

____

____

____

____

____

____

____

____

____

____

____

3 things I am thankful for today:

1.____________________

2.____________________

3.____________________

What is one thing God wants me to do for Him today?

____

He Knows the Outcome

"You guide me with your counsel, and afterward you will take me into glory."

Psalm 73:24

How great we have it! As believers, we have direct access to God's advice and counsel for small and big decisions. How could we possibly go wrong! Unless, of course, we choose to ignore it! Don't go against His advice – He knows the outcome already!

~Warren W.

3 things I am thankful for today:

1.____________________

2.____________________

3.____________________

What is one thing God wants me to do for Him today?

A Strong Wind Blowing

God's breath created the universe, the world, and everything in it. His breath also created the Bible. Want to get to know our Lord better? God is talking to us.

"The Bible is not a book to be read, It is a book to be heard." -d.c.sprawls

~Diane G.

"All Scripture is God-breathed and is useful for teaching, rebuking, correcting and training in righteousness, so that the servant of God may be thoroughly equipped for every good work."

2 Timothy 3:16-17

3 things I am thankful for today:

1.____________________

2.____________________

3.____________________

What is one thing God wants me to do for Him today?

The Most Important Things

"A good name is more desirable than great riches; to be esteemed is better than silver or gold."

Proverbs 22:1

Who do we look up to? What do we teach our children to value most? Many problems in our world today come from the fact that we have lost our way. We need to remember and pass on what should be most important for us, our heirs, and our world!

~Dotti K.

3 things I am thankful for today:

1.____________________

2.____________________

3.____________________

What is one thing God wants me to do for Him today?

Whom or What Do I Worship?

I'd never worship a golden calf, but other false idols in life can easily focus attention away from God. Social media is so addictive that I can easily spend precious time on my smart phone or laptop, as well as giving too much attention on books, games, and television. We should identify the false idols preventing us from listening for God.

~Sharon B.

"You shall have no other Gods before me."
Exodus 20:3

3 things I am thankful for today:

1.____________________

2.____________________

3.____________________

What is one thing God wants me to do for Him today?

Love in Action

"'A new command I give you: Love one another. As I have loved you, so you must love one another.'"

John 13:34

Love shows in behavior towards others. Love is not just talk but action, in what we do or don't do for others. Showing love and compassion in the way we speak and act towards others is how we will be judged as Jesus' disciples. What are we showing?

~Tanya J.

3 things I am thankful for today:

1.____________________

2.____________________

3.____________________

What is one thing God wants me to do for Him today?

Obedience for God's Glory

Obedience is a voluntary act to put oneself under another's authority. Jesus put Himself under God the Father's control. He voluntarily allowed others to lead Him along the punishing path to the cross for our salvation, and God's glory. Are we willing to relinquish our thoughts, emotions, and attitude for someone else's good, and for God's glory?

~Ruth N.

"Son though he was, he learned obedience from what he suffered"
Hebrews 5:8

3 things I am thankful for today:

1.____________

2.____________

3.____________

What is one thing God wants me to do for Him today?

3. Servant Leadership – A New Creation

by Warren Walters

Around noon on February 3, 2010, I gave the doctor permission to remove my wife from life support. It was the final act in Maria's life-long struggle with health issues. The doctor fought all night to save her like one of God's chosen warriors, but the odds were stacked against them both. At that fateful moment, I felt like I had killed her.

The evening before, Maria and I didn't say goodbye; we just smiled as they wheeled her away for open heart surgery number six. I told her I'd be waiting for her when she woke up. She never did.

Next, I had to face Maria's elderly parents, Leonidas and Teresa, and tell them what I had done. Adding to the difficulty was they spoke limited English, and I spoke almost no Spanish. Maria had been our translator. I suddenly realized I was now "stuck" with them. And I resented it!

How could I wallow in my own self pity, grovel in my own grief, immerse myself in my own misery when I had to indulge them in theirs…look after them…cater to their needs? It wasn't fair, and I resented it!

At the time, I had God in my life, but didn't know Jesus, much less asking Him to be my personal savior. I was still walking in the flesh, and as we all know, resentment is on the top shelf of "fleshly" sins.

As I was their only family in Arkansas and they were my only family in this country, they were my responsibility. Due to language and custom barriers, they were pretty helpless, so it was the right thing to do. However, since it interfered with my own selfish woes (no time to get a good wallow on), I resented it.

The following year, Leonidas became ill and died at home. Teresa called me first. She needed me to handle arrangements on her behalf, and I resented it. The attendant sent to remove his body had no assistant, so I had to help him move the body to the gurney. And I resented it!

In August 2011, Gail entered my life, and things began to brighten. Over time, I was introduced to God's Son and began to see things differently – slowly at first, but emphatically different. However, Teresa resented Gail. Big time!

As Teresa's health declined, I became increasingly involved in her everyday life and, try as I might, I could not help resenting it some, particularly because I wanted to feel free to enjoy the renewal I was experiencing.

Eventually, I had to take Teresa's car away as she could no longer drive safely, which meant she had to rely on me even more. And I resented it!

Finally, after her second stroke, Teresa had to be relocated to an assisted living facility. Although she missed being in her own home, she tried to make the best of it. Every day for the last three years of her life, I drove down after Pickleball to visit Teresa. We would sit the sunshine and watch the people and traffic until her lunch time and then I would go home.

Finally, at 6:00 a.m. on New Year's Day 2018, I received a call from the facility that dear Teresa had passed away. I was finally free of my obligation – and I resented it!

Only God can turn resentment into love.

> *"Therefore, if anyone is in Christ, the new creation has come: The old has gone, the new is here!"* 2 Corinthians 5:17
>
> *"I do not understand what I do. For what I want to do I do not do, but what I hate I do."* Romans 7:15

Putting God First

"If God is not first in my thoughts, my finances, my family, my everything, then God is not first in my life." Think about this: we can build a wall with the bricks thrown at us in life OR we can build a road. Choose to walk that road to the only Person who can truly bring you the comfort and peace you so desperately long for. It's up to you.

~Peggy H.

"'Love the Lord your God with all your heart and with all your soul and with all your mind.' This is the first and greatest commandment. And the second is like it: 'Love your neighbor as yourself.'"

Matthew 22:37-40

3 things I am thankful for today:

1.________________

2.________________

3.________________

What is one thing God wants me to do for Him today?

For Us

"For God so loved the world that he gave his one and only Son, that whoever believes in him shall not perish but have eternal life."

John 3:16

Our world seems crazy at times. We may ask, "Does God really love us?" YES!! For us, He sent His son, Jesus, to take on all of our sins. For us, Jesus suffered and died. For us, God provided a way that our sins are forgiven. For us, we have eternal life by believing in Jesus. That's immeasurable love!

~Debbie R.

3 things I am thankful for today:

1.________________

2.________________

3.________________

What is one thing God wants me to do for Him today?

The Devil Prowls

The power of praying for our family and friends is life-changing. God only wants good for us all, but the evil one plots and schemes against us. Instead of just worrying, we need to cover them in prayer every day. A prayer journal can help us keep track of prayer concerns and answered prayers. Looking back over past prayer requests strengthens our faith.

~Sharon B.

"Be alert and of sober mind. Your enemy the devil prowls around like a roaring lion looking for someone to devour."

1 Peter 5:8

3 things I am thankful for today:

1.____________________

2.____________________

3.____________________

What is one thing God wants me to do for Him today?

Which Do You Feed?

"I do not understand what I do. For what I want to do I do not do, but what I hate I do."

Romans 7:15

I've heard this quoted many times, but have no idea who to credit:

Two natures beat within my breast
The one is foul; the one is blessed
The one I love. The one I hate.
The one I feed will dominate.
Author Unknown

Feast on Christ!

~Vickie H.

3 things I am thankful for today:

1.____________________

2.____________________

3.____________________

What is one thing God wants me to do for Him today?

No Condemnation

Today, this day, we believers in Jesus, are NOT condemned. We can experience freedom from the weight of sin and guilt, right now! What a weight off our back!

~Julie K

"Therefore, there is now no condemnation for those who are in Christ Jesus."

Romans 8:1

3 things I am thankful for today:

1.__________

2.__________

3.__________

What is one thing God wants me to do for Him today?

Act On It

"for it is God who works in you to will and to act in order to fulfill his good purpose."
Philippians 2:13

Have you ever been inspired to do something good for someone? That thought did not come from the evil one, but from God. We should obey and act on His promptings.

~Teela Y.

3 things I am thankful for today:

1.________________________

2.________________________

3.________________________

What is one thing God wants me to do for Him today?

Choose Your Friends Wisely

No matter where we are, it seems there are people who like to stir up trouble. Sometimes, they even tell lies about us or other people. If we allow it, they will take up space in our heads to the point that we become ill. For our own health and peace of mind we must avoid them.

~Steve B.

"I urge you, brothers and sisters, to watch out for those who cause divisions and put obstacles in your way that are contrary to the teaching you have learned. Keep away from them."

Romans 16:17

____
____
____
____
____
____
____
____
____
____
____
____
____
____
____
____
____

3 things I am thankful for today:

1.____________________________

2.____________________________

3.____________________________

What is one thing God wants me to do for Him today?

____

Pathways

"Trust in the Lord with all your heart and lean not on your own understanding; in all your ways submit to him, and he will make your paths straight."

Proverbs 3:5-6

We should not try to solve all our problems ourselves. We must have confidence in the Lord and follow His paths. He has all of the answers that we may not understand or want to follow. As Christians, we must have faith and know that He is God.

~Donna P.

3 things I am thankful for today:

1.________________________

2.________________________

3.________________________

What is one thing God wants me to do for Him today?

Our Purpose

God's purpose for us may not be clear, but a good starting point is to ask for His guidance and direction. The old Yiddish proverb, "We plan, God laughs," is a truth we ignore at our own peril. Many of us in the Village feel God put us here for a reason. Ask Him why.

~Rita T.

"Many are the plans in a person's heart, but it is the Lord's purpose that prevails."

Proverbs 19:21

3 things I am thankful for today:

1.____________________

2.____________________

3.____________________

What is one thing God wants me to do for Him today?

Still I Follow

"'Come, follow me,' Jesus said, 'and I will send you out to fish for people.'"

Matthew 4:19

I'm not a great fisherman, but even I know that fish simply do not want to be caught! As I follow Jesus, some will not be interested in joining this walk of discipleship. But still I follow, and I pray Jesus will use me in just the right way to touch another life and make an impact for Him.

~Rev. Chris H.

3 things I am thankful for today:

1.____________________

2.____________________

3.____________________

What is one thing God wants me to do for Him today?

God's First Question

God's question to Adam, "Where are you?" was more than hide-and-seek. God's question to us is, "Where are you...in your soul, in your relationship to me, in your relationship to your family and loved ones, in your spiritual life, in your response to all of creation... and where are you in response to my command to love one another?"

~Jim H.

"But the Lord God called to the man, 'Where are you?' He answered, 'I heard you in the garden, and I was afraid because I was naked; so I hid.' And he said, 'Who told you that you were naked? Have you eaten from the tree that I commanded you not to eat from?'"

Genesis 3:9-11

3 things I am thankful for today:

1.____________________

2.____________________

3.____________________

What is one thing God wants me to do for Him today?

Why Must We Endure Trials?

"Consider it pure joy, my brothers and sisters, whenever you face trials of many kinds, because you know that the testing of your faith produces perseverance. Let perseverance finish its work so that you may be mature and complete, not lacking anything."

James 1:2-4

So, are we persecuted for our beliefs? I say yes – not in the sense of death or imprisonment, but through hate manifested by ridicule and isolation. Just as Jesus was hated for who He was, so we will face what He faced. How do we deal with haters? The same way He did – with LOVE! Through our confidence in Him, we step out in joy.

~Diane G.

3 things I am thankful for today:

1.____________________

2.____________________

3.____________________

What is one thing God wants me to do for Him today?

New Day

Each day we wake up is a new day! How does God want to use us today? How can we be a blessing to someone else today? Try a simple smile, a word of encouragement, or a kind gesture when not expected. May God shine His love and light through us to be a blessing to others.

~Nancy M.

"The Lord has done it this very day; let us rejoice today and be glad."

Psalm 118:24

3 things I am thankful for today:

1.____________________

2.____________________

3.____________________

What is one thing God wants me to do for Him today?

You Will Be Blessed

"You will be blessed when you come in and blessed when you go out."
Deuteronomy 28:6

Before the inside sheet rock was hung in our new home, a variety of Bible verses were placed inside the walls and over the door frames. Each room has a reminder that God is in our home. When you come in or go out, you are blessed.

~Vicki F.

3 things I am thankful for today:

1.____________________

2.____________________

3.____________________

What is one thing God wants me to do for Him today?

Stinkin' Thinkin'

Isn't it a blessing to have a heavenly Father who knows when we need an attitude adjustment? When we get in that worry mode, or that "feeling inadequate" mode, or that just downright complaining mode, He provides an answer. He tells us what to think about, for His peace. Think on that.

~Becky M.

"Finally, brothers and sisters, whatever is true, whatever is noble, whatever is right, whatever is pure, whatever is lovely, whatever is admirable–if anything is excellent or praiseworthy–think about such things. Whatever you have learned or received or heard from me, or seen in me–put it into practice. And the God of peace will be with you."

Philippians 4:8-9

3 things I am thankful for today:

1.____________________

2.____________________

3.____________________

What is one thing God wants me to do for Him today?

Lukewarm

"So, because you are lukewarm—neither hot nor cold—I am about to spit you out of my mouth."

Revelation 3:16

A lukewarm drink doesn't satisfy our thirst. We may even want to spit it out. May we never be found cold, lukewarm, or indifferent toward God. We don't want to settle for following God halfway. It takes work to keep our flame burning brightly each and every day, but the Lord helps us.

~Chris C.

3 things I am thankful for today:

1.____________________

2.____________________

3.____________________

What is one thing God wants me to do for Him today?

Travel Mercies

Retirement is a new stage in life for each of us in our beautiful Village. It can mean new friends and time to explore., but also requires us to re-evaluate many things we previously thought essential. What a comforting assurance for those of us who face new and untried experiences!

~Patty M.

"the Lord will watch over your coming and going both now and forevermore."

Psalm 121:8

3 things I am thankful for today:

1.____________________

2.____________________

3.____________________

What is one thing God wants me to do for Him today?

Life on the Lake

"'And God said, "Let the water teem with living creatures, and let birds fly above the earth across the vault of the sky."'

Genesis 1:20

On July 7th, 1966, a less than honorable grandmother gave her non-church-going granddaughter *The Bible Story Book, Volume 1*. The little girl's imagination was captured by a picture of trees, water, and birds of all kinds. Now, at age 61, that girl lives on the bank of Lake Cortez and daily witnesses the creation – and loves that Creator. Sometimes, God uses the most unsuspecting subjects to plant seeds for the Kingdom.

~Reba L.

3 things I am thankful for today:

1.________________________

2.________________________

3.________________________

What is one thing God wants me to do for Him today?

Pretty is as Pretty Does

How we are drawn to "pretty people!" Pretty eyes, pretty hair, size 4's! My mother used to tell me, "Pretty is as pretty does..." I think that was her interpretation of 1 Samuel 16:7 – our Lord looks at the heart. What if we spent more time developing a loving heart?

~Vickie H.

"But the Lord said to Samuel, 'Do not consider his appearance or his height, for I have rejected him. The Lord does not look at the things people look at. People look at the outward appearance, but the Lord looks at the heart.'"

1 Samuel 16:7

3 things I am thankful for today:

1.________________

2.________________

3.________________

What is one thing God wants me to do for Him today?

No Wisdom Nor Understanding

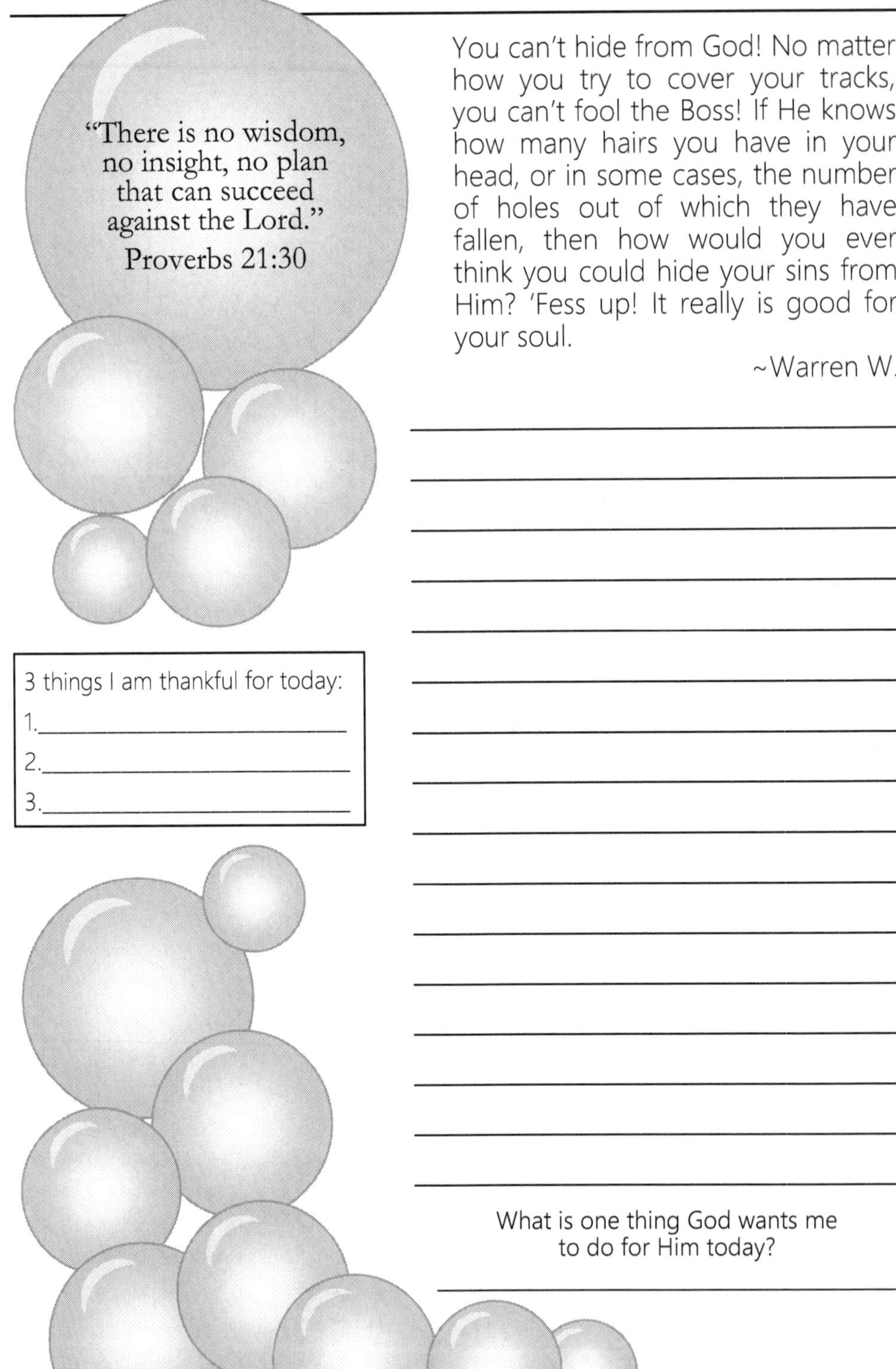

"There is no wisdom, no insight, no plan that can succeed against the Lord."
Proverbs 21:30

You can't hide from God! No matter how you try to cover your tracks, you can't fool the Boss! If He knows how many hairs you have in your head, or in some cases, the number of holes out of which they have fallen, then how would you ever think you could hide your sins from Him? 'Fess up! It really is good for your soul.

~Warren W.

3 things I am thankful for today:

1.____________________

2.____________________

3.____________________

What is one thing God wants me to do for Him today?

Eternal Life

God never promised believers an easy life nor one without hardships, but we can be confident and assured that He has promised us an eternal life with Him forever.

~Julie K.

"And this is what he promised us– eternal life."

1 John 2:25

3 things I am thankful for today:

1.____________________

2.____________________

3.____________________

What is one thing God wants me to do for Him today?

Clearing Mary Magdalene

"...The Twelve were with him, and also some women who had been cured of evil spirits and diseases: Mary (called Magdalene) from whom seven demons had come out...and many others. These women were helping to support them out of their own means."

Luke 8:1-3

This glimpse of Mary Magdalene does not imply that she was a former prostitute. The evil spirits could be any number of illnesses, physical or mental, but do not connote sexual sin. Mary Magdalene and many other women supported Jesus out of their own resources, indicating they all were independent women of some means – yet another example of how Jesus was ahead of His time in giving value to women.

~Paula D.

____

____

____

____

____

____

____

____

____

____

____

____

____

____

____

3 things I am thankful for today:

1.______________________________

2.______________________________

3.______________________________

What is one thing God wants me to do for Him today?

____

God Turns Tears Into Praise

David testified of God's workings during his grief. We will never understand how, but know God still works in grieving families today. God has sympathy and empathy for physical pain and emotional suffering, for He too suffered the death of His child. Remember, cry, but also praise God while grieving. Trust Him to cover you with His peaceful joy.

~Ruth N.

"You turned my wailing into dancing; you removed my sackcloth and clothed me with joy, that my heart may sing your praises and not be silent. Lord my God, I will praise you forever."

Psalm 30:11-12

3 things I am thankful for today:

1.______________________

2.______________________

3.______________________

What is one thing God wants me to do for Him today?

God Equips the Called

"Then I heard the voice of the Lord saying, 'Whom shall I send? And who will go for us?' And I said, 'Here am I. Send me!'"

Isaiah 6:8

Weeks after our 2000 wedding, Steve surprised me by wanting to attend a "Discerning the Call" conference. Both filled with doubt, we attended all sessions. At closing, as we sang *Here I Am, Lord,* it was clear that he was being called as a local pastor. In a leap of faith, he retired from his state job to enter preparation. And I was called to be the pastor's wife!

~Sharon B.

3 things I am thankful for today:

1.____________________

2.____________________

3.____________________

What is one thing God wants me to do for Him today?

Charity

A tornado came oh, so close to touching down in Hot Springs Village, blocking streets with twisted trees, peeling off roofs, and tossing boats like bathtub toys. Volunteer response was immediate and amazing! Lord, thank You for neighbors' helping one another, just as Jesus instructed.

~Chris S.

"Carry each other's burdens, and in this way you will fulfill the law of Christ."

Galatians 6:2

3 things I am thankful for today:

1.__________

2.__________

3.__________

What is one thing God wants me to do for Him today?

A Father's Responsibility

"And, ye fathers, provoke not your children to wrath: but bring them up in the nurture and admonition of the Lord."

Ephesians 6:4 (KJV)

God intended that fathers rear their children, to educate and train (nurture) them, to exhort and direct them to God. Too many homes have no father around. Children hear promises that are never kept. They grow up with domestic violence. What a different society we would have today if fathers took this responsibility to heart.

~Suzan R.

3 things I am thankful for today:

1.____________________

2.____________________

3.____________________

What is one thing God wants me to do for Him today?

Give Us Strength

If there is something God wants us to do and we study His word, the Holy Spirit will refresh us and we will have the strength to accomplish God's work. So, let's practice getting up each morning to study His word, listen, and do our best to serve Him.

~Tanya J.

"but those who hope in the Lord will renew their strength. They will soar on wings like eagles; they will run and not grow weary, they will walk and not be faint."

Isaiah 40:31

3 things I am thankful for today:

1.____________________

2.____________________

3.____________________

What is one thing God wants me to do for Him today?

Pruning Hurts

"He cuts off every branch in me that bears no fruit, while every branch that does bear fruit he prunes so that it will be even more fruitful."

John 15:2

There comes a time in our lives where we just might need to "prune" unwanted things like a bad habit, a poor attitude, or a short temper. Pruning hurts, but from new growth comes beauty and refreshment.

~Peggy H.

3 things I am thankful for today:

1.____________________

2.____________________

3.____________________

What is one thing God wants me to do for Him today?

Making All Things New

To do anything worthwhile, it's important to see the end before you ever begin. That is why Jesus's example is the very best we can have – He knew the end of the story before He ever came to this earth! He died (for us!); He rose, and we will live with Him in Eternity. No ifs, ands, or buts.

~Vickie H.

"He who was seated on the throne said, 'I am making everything new!' Then he said, 'Write this down, for these words are trustworthy and true.'"

Revelation 21:5

3 things I am thankful for today:

1.__________

2.__________

3.__________

What is one thing God wants me to do for Him today?

How Great Thou Art

"In a loud voice they were saying: 'Worthy is the Lamb, who was slain, to receive power and wealth and wisdom and strength and honor and glory and praise!'"

Revelation 5:12

Jesus only lived on earth for 33 years. He never traveled more than 100 miles from His home. Yet. Charles Lamb was right in saying, "If all the illustrious men of history were gathered together, and Shakespeare should enter their presence, they would rise to do him honor; but if Jesus Christ should come in, they would fall down and worship Him."

~Kathy S.

3 things I am thankful for today:

1.____________________

2.____________________

3.____________________

What is one thing God wants me to do for Him today?

You Are Beautiful

I am altogether beautiful when God resides in me. Our culture today does not determine my beauty. I don't have to look a certain way, live in an awesome house, say the right words. God looks at what's in my heart. He loves me the way He made me. How could that not be good enough for me?

~Debbie R.

"You are altogether beautiful, my darling; there is no flaw in you."

Song of Songs 4:7

3 things I am thankful for today:

1.____________________

2.____________________

3.____________________

What is one thing God wants me to do for Him today?

4. Rock Bottom

by Susan Viles

"Rock bottom will teach you lessons that mountain tops never will." ~Unknown

Our new life was in disarray. We had left all of our family and friends in Woodward, Oklahoma. We were not even totally unpacked and had lots of home-improvement projects. So, when the NewComers Class began, there was no doubt in my mind it was for me.

A small group of NewComers began meeting at one member's beautiful lake home for cooking classes. Cooking wasn't my thing, but our illustrious host was determined to melt chocolate in her restaurant-style sauce pan, while letting ingredients set and rise before putting the mix in one of her four ovens. We continued to watch as she created pieces of art from her five -page recipes. All the while, we drank orange juice and enjoyed pastries, laughing and sharing stories of our families, our former homes, and our interests. Fun!

The perfect morning came to a screeching halt when my cell phone rang; the name on the caller ID was my son-in-law's. He told me that my 28-year-old daughter had just been diagnosed with cancer.

I was in shock! Kara had several warning symptoms and was scheduled for a colonoscopy, but was then told, "A colonoscopy would not be beneficial at this time." A year later, we were dealing with cancer at an advanced stage.

My new friends saw me shaking. When I explained why, a circle of prayer formed immediately. We lifted Kara (and me!) up to our Lord. Then, I rushed home to pack. My husband and I were off bright and early the next morning for the eight-hour trip.

Over the next four months, I traveled often between Arkansas and Oklahoma to "be there" for my daughter and her family through a very aggressive chemo. Life has been a nightmarish roller coaster ever since. After chemo, came the torturous six weeks of daily radiation in Memorial Sloan Kettering Cancer Center in New York City. Kara and I missed our loved ones and "normal" lives. After two months of recovery from the side effects of radiation, Kara faced a major surgery which changed her quality of life forever.

During the healing reprieve, we took a family vacation, escaping to the beaches of Mexico where Kara was married 11 years earlier. Her sisters and their husbands were with us as we laughed, snorkeled, ziplined, relaxed, and basked in the sun. We all tried our best to not think about or talk about the big "C."

The outpouring of love in so many different caring ways and by so many dear friends has been overwhelming. The new friends God has brought into our lives supported us in ways I never dreamed possible – prayers, calls, texts, emails, and constant reminders that we are part of the Body of Christ. My heart was shattered by fear and pain; their prayer covering sustained me from day to day!

God has been with us every step of the way opening doors. One great example: Hope Lodge of NYC has provided shelter for us during our many trips to NYC for treatments. We cannot say enough good things about healthcare experts at Memorial Sloan Kettering Cancer Center. Kara truly has a wonderful team of caring, expert oncologists.

Kara's (and our) life will never be the same. We try not to ask, "Why?" but, "What?" What can we learn from this horrible experience? We have no idea what tomorrow holds, but we know Who holds our hand.

We covet all of your prayers.

> *"'The Lord himself goes before you and will be with you; he will never leave you nor forsake you. Do not be afraid; do not be discouraged.'"* Deuteronomy 31:8
>
> *"Not only so, but we also glory in our sufferings, because we know that suffering produces perseverance;"* Romans 5:3

Jars of Clay

Jesus in us is our treasure. Whether our days have tears or sadness, may others see love in our eyes, smiles on our faces, and hear kindness in our voices. Each day is a divine assignment to share our treasure with others. May others see Jesus in us as we bear fruit that brings Him glory.

~Chris C.

"But we have this treasure in jars of clay to show that this all-surpassing power is from God and not from us."

2 Corinthians 4:7

3 things I am thankful for today:

1.____________________

2.____________________

3.____________________

What is one thing God wants me to do for Him today?

He Knows Us

"When I consider your heavens, the work of your fingers, the moon and the stars, which you have set in place, what is mankind that you are mindful of them, human beings that you care for them?"

Psalm 8:3-4

It's amazing really. The universe as we know it continues to grow as we gain stronger lenses for our telescopes. And yet, for the vastness of this creation – both seen and unseen – God knows us by name. God loves us. God's Spirit dwells in us. How incredible a gift is the Father's love for us!

~Rev. Chris H.

3 things I am thankful for today:

1.____________________

2.____________________

3.____________________

What is one thing God wants me to do for Him today?

Don't Fear Satan's Darkness

Yesterday, while taking a shower in our windowless bathroom, the electricity went out. As I fumbled in the dark, a thin ray of light from an emergency light shone through the doorway crack, giving enough light to safely get out of the shower. Remember, while living in our dark sinful world, God's illumination always shines to guide our steps.

~Ruth N.

"The Lord is my light and my salvation–whom shall I fear? The Lord is the stronghold of my life–of whom shall I be afraid?"

Psalm 27:1

3 things I am thankful for today:

1.________________

2.________________

3.________________

What is one thing God wants me to do for Him today?

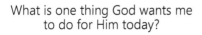

Shine On

"'the Lord make his face shine on you and be gracious to you; the Lord turn his face toward you and give you peace.'"

Numbers 6:25-26

When we spend time worshiping God, we shine from within. We can't look sad or grumpy when we are giving God praise. The more we worship God, the happier and more content we will be, knowing that He is watching over us, always loving and supporting us in both the good and bad times.

~Tanya J.

3 things I am thankful for today:

1.____________________

2.____________________

3.____________________

What is one thing God wants me to do for Him today?

Promises You Can Bank On

The Bible is God's Book of Promises – and we all know that God never breaks a promise. Every promise He has made to us is written down, irrevocable, collectible, ready to be honored, and fully guaranteed. All we have to do is believe in Him, have the faith, put our trust in Him, and enjoy the gift of God's grace and His Book of Promises.

~Warren W.

"Come to me, all you who are weary and burdened, and I will give you rest."
Matthew 11:28

3 things I am thankful for today:

1.____________________

2.____________________

3.____________________

What is one thing God wants me to do for Him today?

God's Purpose Will Stand

"Remember the former things, those of long ago; I am God, and there is no other; I am God, and there is none like me. I make known the end from the beginning, from ancient times, what is still to come. I say, 'My purpose will stand, and I will do all that I please.'"

Isaiah 46: 9-10

On May 15, 2015, the accidental death of our 5½ year old great grandson suffocated my body with shock, numbness, and unbelievable grief. But in my soul I heard, "this is no surprise to God." Even with a broken heart, I knew God had a purpose for Benjamin's short years here on Earth. With great pain I could only say, "Not mine, but Your will be done, Lord."

~Ruth N.

3 things I am thankful for today:

1.________________________

2.________________________

3.________________________

What is one thing God wants me to do for Him today?

Unlimited Power and Grace

God tells us that we can move mountains, but He doesn't say we can do it by ourselves! He says if we have faith in His unlimited power and grace, then we can achieve what would otherwise be impossible! Don't limit your possibilities, believe and achieve!

~Vickie H.

"Jesus looked at them and said, 'With man this is impossible, but with God all things are possible.'"
Matthew 19:26

3 things I am thankful for today:

1.____________________

2.____________________

3.____________________

What is one thing God wants me to do for Him today?

The Perfect Love

"Then they can urge the younger women to love their husbands and children, to be self-controlled and pure, to be busy at home, to be kind, and to be subject to their husbands, so that no one will malign the word of God."

Titus 2: 4-5

The kind of love that God calls us to isn't conditional or based upon feelings. This kind of love isn't the kind that you can "fall out" of. It isn't an optional love, it's a commandment. True love grows and strengthens over time as we are obedient to God's instruction.

~Jody M.

3 things I am thankful for today:

1.____________________

2.____________________

3.____________________

What is one thing God wants me to do for Him today?

Neither Poverty Nor Riches

I've always said that the only time money is really important is when you don't have it. Poverty breeds worry, oppression, and can lead to personal problems. Likewise, when things are going great, we may tend to depend on ourselves more than God. Rest on faith; He will provide.

~Vickie H.

"give me neither poverty nor riches, but give me only my daily bread."
Proverbs 30:8

3 things I am thankful for today:

1.____________________

2.____________________

3.____________________

What is one thing God wants me to do for Him today?

The Power!

"Therefore confess your sins to each other and pray for each other so that you may be healed. The prayer of a righteous person is powerful and effective."
James 5:16

We must be clean before God for our prayers to have clout! Therefore, we must confess our sins – simple to do and easily forgiven! Prayer makes a difference, and I am a firm believer that the more the merrier! We have prayer chains – please contact them for your special intentions. Continue to look for what you can learn and remember, His Will Be Done! GOD listens!

~LunaGram

3 things I am thankful for today:

1.________________

2.________________

3.________________

What is one thing God wants me to do for Him today?

Sweet Words

While I was recovering from surgery, a friend brought a bag of sweet roasted pecans. My doctor came often to offer words of encouragement, making me feel like his star patient. I thought he might be coming just for pecans, but he knew his caring words meant more to me than pecans did to him.

~Teela Y.

"Gracious words are a honeycomb, sweet to the soul and healing to the bones."

Proverbs 16:24

3 things I am thankful for today:

1.____________________

2.____________________

3.____________________

What is one thing God wants me to do for Him today?

Think to Thank

"I will praise you, Lord, with all my heart; before the 'gods' I will sing your praise."
Psalm 138:1

The difference between think and thank is one little vowel. The two words are interrelated. Ingratitude is always the result of thoughtlessness. For example, think of all the small kindnesses you receive from a special neighbor and thank them. Then find someone else to whom you can return kindnesses.

~Patty M.

3 things I am thankful for today:

1.____________________

2.____________________

3.____________________

What is one thing God wants me to do for Him today?

Stay Focused

As I spend time with the Lord, my thoughts tend to jump ahead to today's plans and problems. I have to remind myself to bring my mind back to the Lord for refreshment and renewal. I will let Him soak into me and focus harder on my time with Him.

~Donna P.

"Look to the Lord and his strength; seek his face always."

Psalm 105:4

3 things I am thankful for today:

1.____________________

2.____________________

3.____________________

What is one thing God wants me to do for Him today?

Comfort Comes

"Blessed are those that mourn, for they will be comforted."

Matthew 5:4

There are times so dark that you think you will never see the light again. But it will come again – slowly and gently.

~Kathy S.

3 things I am thankful for today:

1.____________________

2.____________________

3.____________________

What is one thing God wants me to do for Him today?

His Purpose for Me!

My eyes were on the clock. He *always* walked through the door at 6:00pm at week's end. 6:30. 7:30. I watched for his headlights. Then, I saw two sets of lights. The sheriff and his chaplain came to tell me about his fatal accident on a rain-slick road. We had so many plans. But it was the Lord's purpose that prevailed.

~JoNancy S.

"Many are the plans in a person's heart, but it is the Lord's purpose that prevails."

Proverbs 19:21

3 things I am thankful for today:

1.__________

2.__________

3.__________

What is one thing God wants me to do for Him today?

In the Face of Challenge

"'Have I not commanded you? Be strong and courageous. Do not be afraid; do not be discouraged, for the Lord your God will be with you wherever you go.'"

Joshua1:9

How do we muster courage in the face of grave difficulties? Fear can easily envelop us in our human frailty. Understanding the great love that the Lord has for us is a first step to faith, and faith leads to a steadfast confidence that no matter what the circumstance, you are not alone. This is grace!

~Rose F.

3 things I am thankful for today:

1.________________________

2.________________________

3.________________________

What is one thing God wants me to do for Him today?

He Does It All

God is responsible! He calls you to be His child; if He has called you, you can know that He loves you. No question about that. If He has called you, He Himself is keeping you. Your future is secure with Him. What joy and peace this brings us. He called because He loves, and He keeps! Simple, profound truth.

~Marilyn C.

"…to those who have been called, who are loved in God the Father and kept for Jesus Christ:…"

Jude 1:1

3 things I am thankful for today:

1.____________________

2.____________________

3.____________________

What is one thing God wants me to do for Him today?

He Lifts Me Up

"but those who hope in the Lord will renew their strength. They will soar on wings like eagles; they will run and not grow weary, they will walk and not be faint."

Isaiah 40:31

Looking back on troubled times, I sometimes wonder how I made it through. I could not have done it on my own strength. Jesus has held me up when I would stumble, strengthening me through prayer time, Christian music, devotionals, and good friends. Waiting patiently or making a choice is easier when I am more peaceful.

~Sharon B.

3 things I am thankful for today:

1.____________________

2.____________________

3.____________________

What is one thing God wants me to do for Him today?

Choices

Sometimes we make choices (changes) and sometimes those choices (changes) make us. There are times of doubt, questioning whether the choice (change) was the "right one." God is always doing new things. We need to be open to new circumstances and remain hopeful, accepting, and grateful for the paths before us, no matter how smooth or rocky.

~Linda N.

"'"See, I am doing a new thing! Now it springs up; do you not perceive it? I am making a way in the wilderness and streams in the wasteland.'"

Isaiah 43:19

3 things I am thankful for today:

1.____________________

2.____________________

3.____________________

What is one thing God wants me to do for Him today?

It Makes Me Cry, Too!

"the Spirit of truth. The world cannot accept him, because it neither sees him nor knows him. But you know him, for he lives with you and will be in you."

John 14:17

Reciting the Easter story to my Sunday School preschool class, one precious little girl started crying when I told of Jesus' death on the cross. So, I held her in my arms and said, "If He didn't die this way, He would not be living in you now. Remember, He loves us that much." She smiled. How about you?

~Becky M.

3 things I am thankful for today:

1.____________________

2.____________________

3.____________________

What is one thing God wants me to do for Him today?

God Shows Us the Way

When facing a tough decision, if we ask God for guidance, He will show us the way. He merely asks us to act justly and show mercy as He does toward us! Do you bring God into the equation when you have a difficult choice to make?

~Dotti K.

"He has shown you, O mortal, what is good. And what does the Lord require of you? To act justly and to love mercy and to walk humbly with your God."

Micah 6:8

3 things I am thankful for today:

1.________________________

2.________________________

3.________________________

What is one thing God wants me to do for Him today?

Faith Booster

"With your mighty arm you redeemed your people, the descendants of Jacob and Joseph."
Psalm 77:15

If my faith is at a weak point, reading the Bible reminds that life can be hard, but God is always good. Sacred scripture reveals His wondrous, steadfast love throughout our ancestors' history, timeless proof to trust His ways. We may not get what we want, but He will always fulfill our needs.

~Chris S.

3 things I am thankful for today:

1.____________________

2.____________________

3.____________________

What is one thing God wants me to do for Him today?

Words...What Are They?

How many times have you tried to pray for someone ill (a family member/dear friend), but the words or even what to pray just won't come out? Did Simon know how to heal his family member? No, but he knew Jesus knew just what to do. We can call on Jesus at any time and whisper, "Jesus, help them." That's enough.

~Phillis R.

"Jesus left the synagogue and went to the home of Simon. Now Simon's mother-in-law was suffering from a high fever, and they asked Jesus to help her."

Luke 4:38

3 things I am thankful for today:

1.________________

2.________________

3.________________

What is one thing God wants me to do for Him today?

Pray Before the Storm

"Consider it pure joy, my brothers and sisters, whenever you face trials of many kinds, because you know that the testing of your faith produces perseverance."

James 1:2-3

This scripture doesn't say IF trials come, but whenever trials come. My habit is, when trials come to us, to pray that our family can and will honor God through them. He is so faithful and causes even the greatest trial to be just a bump in the road and not a dead end.

~Reba L.

3 things I am thankful for today:

1.____________________

2.____________________

3.____________________

What is one thing God wants me to do for Him today?

Alas, Woe Is Me!

Think – if you eliminated all your current worries, what would you do with all your new free time? So many of us spend our now worrying about what-ifs. We may not know what's in store for us, but God does! Jesus encourages us to lay our worry at His feet, trusting in His plan for our lives.

~Susan M.

"Can any one of you by worrying add a single hour to your life?"

Matthew 6:27

3 things I am thankful for today:

1.____________________

2.____________________

3.____________________

What is one thing God wants me to do for Him today?

Compare

"Each one should test their own actions. Then they can take pride in themselves alone, without comparing themselves to someone else, for each one should carry their own load."

Galatians 6:4-5

God has a specific plan for us, and we won't accomplish that plan by looking at others. Count your blessings and not the blessings of someone else. Let God control your life and know that all you need is Christ. Set your mind at peace by following the Lord.

~Donna P.

3 things I am thankful for today:

1.________________________

2.________________________

3.________________________

What is one thing God wants me to do for Him today?

Cling Ever So Tightly

An old journal entry of mine says, 'Your desire to live in My presence goes against the grain of the world, the flesh, and the Devil. Much of my weariness results from the constant battle between these awesome opponents." Our only recourse is to clad ourselves in the Armor of God, pray, and cling ever so tightly to His mighty hand! Amen.

~Warren W.

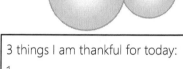

"Since we live by the Spirit, let us keep in step with the Spirit."
Galatians 5:25

3 things I am thankful for today:

1.____________________

2.____________________

3.____________________

What is one thing God wants me to do for Him today?

Speak No Evil

"For whoever would love life and see good days must keep their tongue from evil and their lips from deceitful speech."
1 Peter 3:10

Be careful, little tongue, what you say. Many times, keeping our tongue, not telling lies, and not being deceitful are mentioned in God's word. The tongue has the power to make our day.
~Teela Y.

3 things I am thankful for today:
1.____________________
2.____________________
3.____________________

What is one thing God wants me to do for Him today?

No Peace from This World

The world doesn't give peace, for it has no peace to give. It fights for peace, it negotiates for peace, it manipulates for peace, but there is no ultimate peace in the world. Jesus offers the only true peace to those who trust in Him.

~Kathy S.

"I have told you these things, so that in me you may have peace. In this world you will have trouble. But take heart! I have overcome the world."

John 16:33

3 things I am thankful for today:

1.____________________

2.____________________

3.____________________

What is one thing God wants me to do for Him today?

May It Begin With Me

"He has shown you,
O mortal, what is good.
And what does the Lord
require of you? To act justly
and to love mercy and to
walk humbly with
your God."

Micah 6:8

In a world filled with darkness and chaos, we must remember that each of us shares in responsibility to one another and to our world. Offer justice, love, kindness, walk gently with God and with one another. We can make a Kingdom difference. We can change our world. May it begin with me, today, right now!

~Rev. Chris H.

3 things I am thankful for today:

1._________________________

2._________________________

3._________________________

What is one thing God wants me to do for Him today?

5. The Blessings Bowl®

by Linda Norman

My mother was a true blessing to me and the rest of our family. She was funny, smart, and a great reflection of the love of God. She started and ended each day praying and praising God. In her later years, she had a peace within her that I strive and pray for daily.

My mother became ill while visiting us in Hot Springs Village and, after surgery, and was diagnosed with colon cancer at age 85. She went home to Texas to live with my brother and sister-in-law and begin treatment.

During that time, phone calls and visits were no longer enough for me. With 300 miles between us, I needed to connect with her in every way possible. Then, God opened my heart to make her a Blessings Bowl® (www.blessingsbowl.com), a bowl which you can fill with written thoughts, memories, prayers, poems, and anything else to acknowledge your many blessings.

Each day, I wrote Bible verses, uplifting quotes from famous people, childhood memories, love notes, and corny jokes on brightly colored scrapbook paper. Each "blessing" was placed in a crystal bowl, which I mailed to her, with instructions to read one per day. Of course, she read them all as soon as she received the bowl, but she did put them all back and continued to read one daily.

When I visited her, I found "blessings" in her Bible, on her nightstand, and on her bulletin board so they remained close-by in her sight, mind, and heart.

Her memorial was a beautiful celebration of a life well lived, reflecting her love for the Lord. The chapel was filled with family and friends who loved and admired her. At the end of her service, all were invited to take a "blessing" from her Blessings Bowl®. Even in death, blessings flowed from this sweet woman of God.

It is a tremendous gift to not only remember how blessed I was by my mother and her love, but also to see others read and share her verses, memories, and words of encouragement with each other. I learned later that her grandson taped his verse on the dashboard of his truck. I keep several in my purse, my Bible, and my studio as a loving reminder that God is good all the time. We never know the difference that one small act may have on us and others.

> *"'Give, and it will be given to you. A good measure, pressed down, shaken together and running over, will be poured into your lap. For with the measure you use, it will be measured to you.'"* Luke 6:38
>
> *"All these blessings will come on you and accompany you if you obey the Lord your God:"* Deuteronomy 28:2

Tears Are Precious to Him

When we think about how valuable our tears and suffering, our tossing and turning at night, all our sorrows are, then see God's attentiveness to each one, such a peace comes over us. Have you experienced His comfort and love and a peace that passes all understanding?

~Peggy H.

"Record my misery; list my tears on your scroll–are they not in your record?"

Psalm 56:8

3 things I am thankful for today:

1.__________

2.__________

3.__________

What is one thing God wants me to do for Him today?

Laughter

"There is a time for everything and a season for every activity under heaven...a time to weep and a time to laugh…"

Ecclesiastes 3:1,4

Each month, *Reader's Digest* has a feature titled "Laughter, the Best Medicine." And it truly is! I like to surround myself with people who can make me laugh. But it is important to know when to laugh and when to refrain from laughing. We should never get our laughs at someone else's expense.

~Steve B.

____

____

____

____

____

____

____

____

____

____

____

____

____

____

____

____

____

3 things I am thankful for today:

1.______________________________

2.______________________________

3.______________________________

What is one thing God wants me to do for Him today?

____

As With Eagle's Wings

Here's another inspirational verse when it has been a full and busy day, or even a slow and empty one! Again, hope in the Lord gives me strength, energy, and motivation to continue to pray, to serve, and be grateful for all the blessings I've received.

~Paula D.

"but those who hope in the Lord will renew their strength. They will soar on wings like eagles; they will run and not grow weary, they will walk and not be faint."

Isaiah 40:31

3 things I am thankful for today:

1.____________________

2.____________________

3.____________________

What is one thing God wants me to do for Him today?

My 2:00AM Friend

"I love the Lord, for he heard my voice; he heard my cry for mercy. Because he turned his ear to me, I will call on him as long as I live."

Psalm 116:1-2

I love the Lord for many reasons, but one blessing; He hears my calls. He knows my voice because we've spent both joyful and hard times together. When I call, God greets me with compassion and forgiveness, and listens. Therefore, with such a faithful friend as that, I will continually call on my Lord for as long as I live.

~Ruth N.

3 things I am thankful for today:

1.__________________________

2.__________________________

3.__________________________

What is one thing God wants me to do for Him today?

A Gift Worth Accepting

Work first, then be rewarded. Didn't we grow up learning that work ethic? God's grace doesn't work that way. It's a gift. Something wrapped up in a special package for each one of us. We just need to accept that gift, and through faith we are saved. What a relief I don't have to earn it! What a blessing!

~Debbie R.

"For it is by grace you have been saved, through faith–and this is not from yourselves, it is the gift of God–not by works, so that no one can boast."

Ephesians 2:8-9

3 things I am thankful for today:

1.____________________

2.____________________

3.____________________

What is one thing God wants me to do for Him today?

Remember to Call

"Call to me and I will answer you and tell you great and unsearchable things you do not know."
Jeremiah 33:3

Do you have God on your speed dial? If not, you should! God hears our prayers, and loves to hear from His children. Don't know His number? Just remember Jeremiah 33:3. That's it! Call to me and I will answer you! Why not try it today?

~Rev. Chris H.

3 things I am thankful for today:

1.____________________

2.____________________

3.____________________

What is one thing God wants me to do for Him today?

Don't Compare

Sometimes, I ashamedly look at others and think, "Well, at least I'm not as heavy as she is," or, "Wow, why can't I be as organized as her?" Then, I remember the words of a dear friend who would say to me, "Don't compare; it leads to pride or despair." If we must compare, let's compare ourselves to Christ, who loves without measure.

~Reba L.

"He committed no sin, and no deceit was found in his mouth."

1 Peter 2:22

3 things I am thankful for today:

1.________________

2.________________

3.________________

What is one thing God wants me to do for Him today?

Our Time to Be Generous

"Is it not to share your food with the hungry and to provide the poor wanderer with shelter– when you see the naked, to clothe them, and not to turn away from your own flesh and blood?"

Isaiah 58:7

This passage always makes me want to clean out my closets and pantry, but here in the Village, the last part hits home. How many of us have had to take in our grandchildren and raise them? My heart goes out to those who have opened their hearts and homes to their flesh and blood and raise them! God Bless you!

~LunaGram

3 things I am thankful for today:

1.____________________

2.____________________

3.____________________

What is one thing God wants me to do for Him today?

Great Job! Way to Go!

How does it feel when nobody seems to notice or appreciate your efforts? How does it feel when a friend/parent/teacher comes to you and says "You did a great job! Way to go!" We all need encouragement and, likewise, what we say to others matters! Just as we receive encouragement from God through His Word, He expects us, as His followers, to be encouragers too!

~Vickie H.

"Therefore encourage one another and build each other up, just as in fact you are doing."

1 Thessalonians 5:11

3 things I am thankful for today:

1.________________

2.________________

3.________________

What is one thing God wants me to do for Him today?

Listen

"Be still, and know that I am God;"
Psalm 46:10

Life is busy. There's always something to do, somewhere to go. Let's remember to take time to be still and spend some time with God. Let His peace fill us, let His love overflow us. We're all busy, but our Savior wants to spend time with us because He loves us so much, He gave His life for us.

~Nancy M.

3 things I am thankful for today:

1.____________________

2.____________________

3.____________________

What is one thing God wants me to do for Him today?

Much to Treasure, Much to Ponder

Think of all that Mary saw and heard regarding God's work in her life and the life of Jesus. She took none of it for granted, but let it permeate her heart. We need to do the same thing. God is working and has worked in our lives as well. These later seasons are a great time to think on all He has done. Treasure His workings in the details of your life. Take time to ponder.

~Marilyn C.

"But Mary treasured up all these things and pondered them in her heart."

Luke 2:19

3 things I am thankful for today:

1.__________

2.__________

3.__________

What is one thing God wants me to do for Him today?

God Heals

“who forgives all your sins and heals all your diseases,”
Psalm 103:3

God heals hurt bodies, troubled minds, aching hearts, messed-up lives, and difficult relationships. God says, “When you come into My presence, the healing begins!” Remember, our God can do awesome things. Nothing is too difficult for Him. While He may not take away every hurt, He will always give you what you need to live joyfully – in spite of the hurts. Just ask !

~Peggy H.

3 things I am thankful for today:

1.____________________

2.____________________

3.____________________

What is one thing God wants me to do for Him today?

Heaven Must Be Glorious

Looking at Hot Springs Village with its beautiful forests, lakes, and wildlife is truly a small touch of Heaven. We should remember to thank the Lord daily for the blessings in our life. Won't it be something to see Heaven's perfect surroundings and be embraced in a love that's like nothing we have ever known?

~Tanya J.

"Lord, I love the house where you live, the place where your glory dwells."

Psalm 26:8

3 things I am thankful for today:

1.____________________

2.____________________

3.____________________

What is one thing God wants me to do for Him today?

Pure Motives

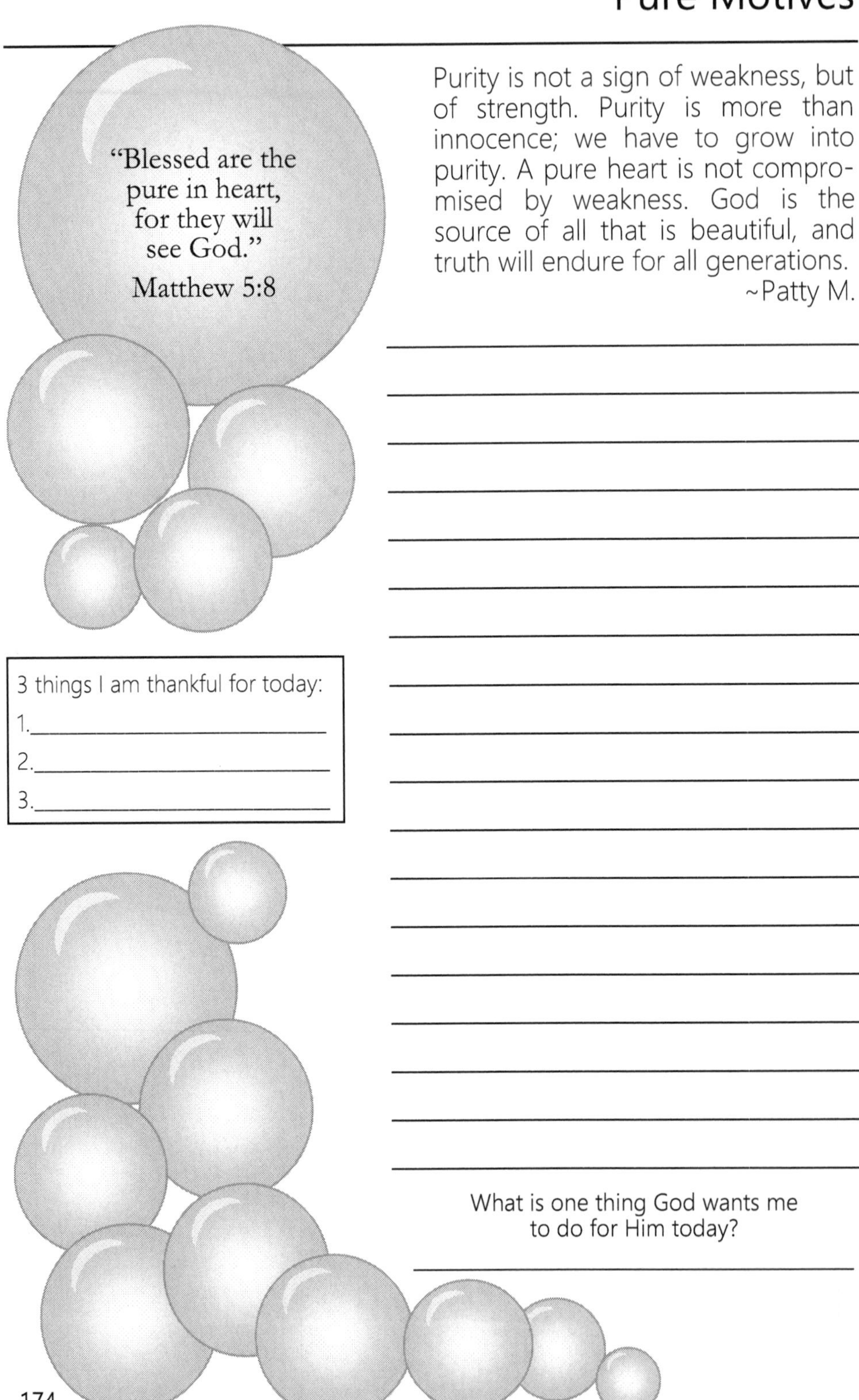

"Blessed are the pure in heart, for they will see God."
Matthew 5:8

Purity is not a sign of weakness, but of strength. Purity is more than innocence; we have to grow into purity. A pure heart is not compromised by weakness. God is the source of all that is beautiful, and truth will endure for all generations.

~Patty M.

3 things I am thankful for today:

1.__________

2.__________

3.__________

What is one thing God wants me to do for Him today?

My Ark Experience

When it comes to Noah and the ark, I'm fascinated by his experience with all creatures gathered into the ark for 40 days and nights. What a lucky person he was! My past 2 years in Hot Springs Village has brought me face to face with many forms of wildlife. I'm thankful to God for choosing Noah and his family to care for all of His creatures.

~Donna P.

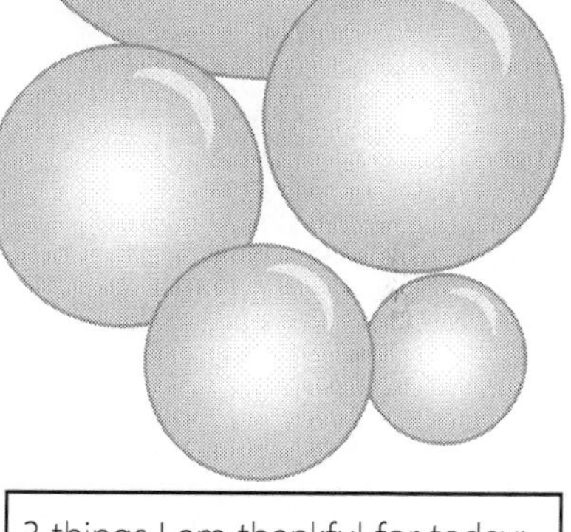

"Pairs of all creatures that have the breath of life in them came to Noah and entered the ark."
Genesis 7:15

3 things I am thankful for today:

1.__________

2.__________

3.__________

What is one thing God wants me to do for Him today?

Progression to Joy

"The Lord is my strength and my shield; my heart trusts in him, and he helps me. My heart leaps for joy, and with my song I praise him"

Psalm 28:7

First, I must with certainty comprehend that God's strength will hold me while living through the trials of life, and believe in the shielding, protective power of Jesus' blood. Then, with no doubts, I'm able to say, "I trust in the Lord." Then, God supplies my needs; my heart overflows with joy, and I gratefully sing praises to my Lord.

~Ruth N.

3 things I am thankful for today:

1.____________________

2.____________________

3.____________________

What is one thing God wants me to do for Him today?

Where's That Verse Found?

Our middle daughter was in the finals of a Bible drill contest when this verse popped into her head. When the judges asked her where the verse was found, she answered, "On the bathroom mirror!" We may write God's word in a journal or on a mirror. May the Lord write His word on our hearts!

~Sue K.

"How good and pleasant it is when God's people live together in unity!"

Psalm 133:1

3 things I am thankful for today:

1.____________________

2.____________________

3.____________________

What is one thing God wants me to do for Him today?

From Wailing to Dancing Again

"You turned my wailing into dancing; you removed my sackcloth and clothed me with joy"

Psalm 30:11

My parents loved to dance. When Dad died in an accident, the dancing ended. Mom lived as a widow for the next 20 years and fondly remembered their dancing days. Then, the day came for her to join Dad in Heaven. Often, when a loved one dies we say, "We lost them." I have not lost them. I know exactly where they are; dancing across heaven.

~Steve B.

3 things I am thankful for today:

1.____________________________

2.____________________________

3.____________________________

What is one thing God wants me to do for Him today?

You Know It's Real

The promise of God's love is real, but just as the total beauty of the ocean cannot be understood until it is seen, so it is with God's love. Until you actually experience it and actually possess it, no one can describe the wonders of His love to you. If not for the love of God, none of us could hope to see Heaven.

~Kathy S.

"The Lord appeared to us in the past, saying: "I have loved you with an everlasting love; I have drawn you with unfailing kindness."

Jeremiah 31:3

3 things I am thankful for today:

1.____________________

2.____________________

3.____________________

What is one thing God wants me to do for Him today?

Always There

"Have I not commanded you? Be strong and courageous. Do not be afraid; do not be discouraged, for the Lord your God will be with you wherever you go.'"

Joshua 1:9

My husband's job moved to a big city having crime problems. I whined my concerned dismay about our young sons' safety to family and friends. Within a month, it was apparent the schools and community were better and safer than the last! A subsequent cross-country move was easier trusting God was going, too.

~Chris S.

3 things I am thankful for today:

1.____________________

2.____________________

3.____________________

What is one thing God wants me to do for Him today?

God's Plan

This verse gives us hope that, even when life gives us lemons instead of lemonade, God has a plan for us. He continues to make us grow until His work is finished and we meet Him face to face. Forget your shortcomings. Remember God's promises. Don't let your present circumstances rob you of joy, but rather may you grow closer to Jesus.

~Chris C.

"But we have this treasure in jars of clay to show that this all-surpassing power is from God and not from us."

2 Corinthians 4:7

3 things I am thankful for today:

1.__________

2.__________

3.__________

What is one thing God wants me to do for Him today?

Wonder, and Be Amazed

"There are three things that are too amazing for me, four that I do not understand: the way of an eagle in the sky, the way of a snake on a rock, the way of a ship on the high seas, and the way of a man with a young woman."

Proverbs 30:18-19

Sometimes Your Word, O Lord, makes me chuckle and reminds me of my place. Four mysteries indeed; not everything can be explained, and there is so much left to wonder. And there are simply some things that will never cease to amaze us! All things bright and beautiful, all creatures great and small...the Lord God made them all!

~Rev. Chris H.

3 things I am thankful for today:

1.____________________

2.____________________

3.____________________

What is one thing God wants me to do for Him today?

A Time and Season for All

Remember that there are seasons in our lives that can help us in transition. It's fruitless to beat ourselves up because we can no longer do something we once enjoyed. Our focus needs to be on our "cans" instead of our "can'ts". The Village offers so many new things to try in our latest season.

~Sharon B.

"There is a time for everything, and a season for every activity under the heavens."

Ecclesiastes 3:1

3 things I am thankful for today:

1.________________

2.________________

3.________________

What is one thing God wants me to do for Him today?

Nature's Proof

"In his hand are the depths of the earth, and the mountain peaks belong to him. The sea is his, for he made it, and his hands formed the dry land. Come, let us bow down in worship, let us kneel before the Lord our Maker;"

Psalm 95:4-6

Have you taken time to revel in nature's beauty? Maybe you've been awestruck by the Bavarian Alps, the Grand Canyon, the Caribbean Sea. Maybe you've marveled at the intricacies of a spider's web, a hummingbird's flight, tiny shells washed up on the beach. God's incredible handiwork can be found everywhere.

~Susan M.

3 things I am thankful for today:

1.____________________

2.____________________

3.____________________

What is one thing God wants me to do for Him today?

Wise Words

I have read that the wise man's lips are called a vessel because they contain and distribute the wisdom that is within. Let's cherish those wise men and women who pour into us. Those who have invested so much in me are Jean Reese, Claudia Petty, Winston Burton, Marion Perkins, Jean Anna Sellars, Yevon Prater and Nancy Yarberry. Oh, to be counted among the wise.

~Reba L.

"Gold there is, and rubies in abundance, but lips that speak knowledge are a rare jewel."

Proverbs 20:15

3 things I am thankful for today:

1.____________________

2.____________________

3.____________________

What is one thing God wants me to do for Him today?

Light of Our Life

"When Jesus spoke again to the people, he said, 'I am the light of the world. Whoever follows me will never walk in darkness, but will have the light of life.'"

John 8 12

Early one morning, as I was walking one of the beautiful trails in the Village, I noticed the light from the sun streaming through the trees onto my shoulders. How blessed we are that the True "Son" shines down upon us each and every day in all that we do and will remain with us for eternity.

~Jody M.

3 things I am thankful for today:

1.____________________

2.____________________

3.____________________

What is one thing God wants me to do for Him today?

Let Go and Let God

Years ago, when my teen was not pleasant to be around, I prayed for peace, that we would not argue during a visit to a camp where he worked. After horseback riding, my son said, "Mom, Jesus has become very real to me this summer!" Wow! Look what I asked God for...and look what a gift He gave me!

~Vickie H.

"Now to him who is able to do immeasurably more than all we ask or imagine, according to his power that is at work within us,"

Ephesians 3:20

3 things I am thankful for today:

1.____________________

2.____________________

3.____________________

What is one thing God wants me to do for Him today?

Naming Stars

"He determines the number of the stars and calls them each by name."

Psalm 147:4

God, our creator, not only knows how many stars He created, but also placed them in the heavens and gave each of them a name. This gives me goosebumps, making me see how I'm a speck compared to the stars, but God knows my name as well, so I'm more than a speck. I am His child.

~Teela Y.

3 things I am thankful for today:

1.____________________

2.____________________

3.____________________

What is one thing God wants me to do for Him today?

Rainy Days

I heard folks grumbling as the rainy days kept coming in Spring 2019 and was reminded of this verse in Hosea. Let us praise God for His refreshing the Village with the much needed moisture. Acknowledge the Lord, and let Him refresh your life as well.

~Peggy H.

"'Let us acknowledge the Lord; let us press on to acknowledge him. As surely as the sun rises, he will appear; he will come to us like the winter rains, like the spring rains that water the earth.'"

Hosea 6:3

3 things I am thankful for today:

1.____________________

2.____________________

3.____________________

What is one thing God wants me to do for Him today?

Marriage: a Battlefield

"So they are no longer two, but one flesh. Therefore what God has joined together, let no one separate."

Matthew 19:6

A plaque saying, "NO LONGER TWO, BUT ONE" hangs in our bathroom as a daily reminder that reflection in the mirror is only half of me. Satan uses his #1 weapon of misunderstanding to separate, but God shows us His character and gives fighting tools against Satan, so that two differently created halves can lovingly live together as one.

~Ruth N.

3 things I am thankful for today:

1.__________________

2.__________________

3.__________________

What is one thing God wants me to do for Him today?

Praises to Our Creator

Too often, I take for granted the uniqueness of how my body operates – how it can heal itself, how I have sufficient oxygen when I run, how my eyes adjust for light. I am in awe of God's wonderful design – it is marvelously complex and could not have been created by happenstance. I will lift up my praises to Him.

~Debbie R.

"I praise you because I am fearfully and wonderfully made; your works are wonderful, I know that full well."

Psalm 139:14

3 things I am thankful for today:

1.________________

2.________________

3.________________

What is one thing God wants me to do for Him today?

6. My Journey in Song

by Suzan Rust

*No other way but to the cross! Without its power, I would be lost. Through all my days, my song will say, come to the cross...no other way.**

How the words of a hymn speak to us! To some, it's the way to salvation. To some, it's peace from a troubled past. To some, it's God's love put to music. To all, it's a beautiful way to praise our Lord and Savior.

We are fortunate to have a Christian hymn writer of our own in the Village. Suzan Rust grew up in a family of gospel music singers. As a child, she had lessons in voice, piano, and flute. She loved music – it was as natural to her as breathing in God's goodness and breathing out beautiful sounds for her Lord.

While her children attended college, Suzan's health began to fail. Doctors told her to just "live with it, because it would only get worse." She begged the Lord to restore her health, but God had other things in store for her.

While Suzan was confined to her home for long periods of time, new gospel songs began to spring from her heart. They found their way to paper and then to the piano. The notes to enhance the God-inspired words came naturally to form beautiful, unique, and inspiring songs – songs which touched the hearts and souls of many hungry church attendees. And, as with all of God's creation, Suzan heard His soft whispers telling her, "Well done, my good and faithful servant!"

Thanks to her daddy, Suzan met Curtis Doss, a former HSV resident, now deceased. Curtis was a famous gospel songwriter, whose works have been sung by the Gaither family and others. One day, Suzan courageously showed Curtis a handwritten copy of a song she had just written. He encouraged her to send it to his publisher and, as they say, the rest is history! Suzan's first song was included in Jeffress/Phillips Music 2001 songbook, and one of Suzan's songs has been in their annual songbook every year since.

*You search for meaning in your life, for answers to this world of strife. When all is vain and all is lost, Come now to Jesus at the cross. No other way but to the cross. Without its power, I would be lost. Through all my days my song will say, Come to the cross...no other way!**

Suzan says, "If God offered me a trade of getting my health back in exchange for the music, I would keep the music. Poor health has given me the opportunity to commune with God through the music He gives me. Glory to His Name!"

"Hear, O ye kings; give ear, O ye princes; I, even I, will sing unto the Lord; I will sing praise to the Lord God of Israel." Judges 5:3 (KJV)

*Lyrics and Melody written by Suzan Watson Rust

My Voice?

In 2007, our son was deployed to Iraq. One of the things that I missed most was getting to talk to him and hear his voice. I would call his cell phone just to listen to his recorded greeting. The Lord reminded me that He loves me and wants to hear my voice in prayer!

~Betty W.

"This, then, is how you should pray: Our Father in heaven, hallowed be your name,"

Matthew 6:9

3 things I am thankful for today:

1.________________

2.________________

3.________________

What is one thing God wants me to do for Him today?

God Gives Time

"Do not be deceived: God cannot be mocked. A man reaps what he sows. Whoever sows to please their flesh, from the flesh will reap destruction; whoever sows to please the Spirit, from the Spirit will reap eternal life."

Galatians 6:7-8

God's truth: each man, woman, boy, and girl is responsible for their own life's decisions. But watching family members self-destruct is very perplexing and exhausting. So, fight Satan's addictive evil with unconditional love, speak God's truth while extending grace, pray, and thank God for His patience, for He does not want anyone to perish in their sin. (2 Peter 3:9)

~Ruth N.

3 things I am thankful for today:

1.____________________

2.____________________

3.____________________

What is one thing God wants me to do for Him today?

God's Not Finished With Me

Every day, I start out tuned into God, but quickly get distracted by life. I endeavor not to be a people-pleaser, not to criticize, not to judge. By noon, I've broken nearly every vow. I thank my God that He allows fresh starts and fresh lessons every hour and every day. By His grace, I am better than I was yesterday, and not as good as I will be tomorrow.

~Sharon B.

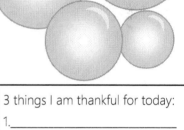

"...he who began a good work in you will carry it on to completion until the day of Christ Jesus."

Philippians 1:6

3 things I am thankful for today:

1.____________________

2.____________________

3.____________________

What is one thing God wants me to do for Him today?

Be a Dazzling Beam of Light!

"In the same way, let your light shine before others, that they may see your good deeds and glorify your Father in heaven."

Matthew 5:16

When you extend kindness, whether by a hug, a smile, a blanket for warmth, some food for the hungry, or clothes for the poor, we are told to do it in such a manner as to give glory to God. Our good deeds, small or large, should exemplify the love of our Heavenly Father and light the way for others to know Him also. As He is light, so we are light. Shine!

~Vickie H.

3 things I am thankful for today:

1.____________________

2.____________________

3.____________________

What is one thing God wants me to do for Him today?

No Matter What

Six months before my husband died, I promised him that I would keep him at home, no matter what. This was the hardest thing I ever had to do. When the time came, he left me with a smile. We both knew that this verse meant exactly what it says, "Nothing would separate us from the love of God!" There was a peace that passes all understanding.

~Phillis R.

"For I am convinced that neither death nor life, neither angels nor demons, neither the present nor the future, nor any powers, neither height nor depth, nor anything else in all creation, will be able to separate us from the love of God that is in Christ Jesus our Lord."

Romans 8:38-39

3 things I am thankful for today:

1.____________________

2.____________________

3.____________________

What is one thing God wants me to do for Him today?

Hear the Word

"The word of the Lord
came to me..."
Jeremiah 1:4

These are some of the most powerful words in scripture for me. When has the word of God come to you? When did you hear God's voice? Are you listening? God still speaks to us. God is here with us. May we answer in faithfulness and expectation!

~Rev. Chris H.

3 things I am thankful for today:

1.____________________

2.____________________

3.____________________

What is one thing God wants me to do for Him today?

Joyful Noise

Visiting priests to our Hot Springs Village church sometimes comment on our "singing" congregation. Perhaps such participation isn't the norm in other Arkansas Catholic communities? Many of us seek God's help, yet may we be just as quick to show joy in praising Him – from whom all blessings flow!

~Chris S.

"Clap your hands, all you nations; shout to God with cries of joy."

Psalm 47:1

3 things I am thankful for today:

1.________________________

2.________________________

3.________________________

What is one thing God wants me to do for Him today?

All Your Effort

"Whatsoever thy hand findeth to do, do it with thy might,..."
Ecclesiastes 9:10 (KJV)

As Christians, God expects us to give all of our ability. Whether as a full-time leader of a church, working a secular job, being a husband or wife, being a child or teenager, or being a parent, God wants us to put all of our effort into everything we do. We are not competing with others, but as a Christians, we should strive to be the best we can be.

~Steve R.

3 things I am thankful for today:

1.____________________

2.____________________

3.____________________

What is one thing God wants me to do for Him today?

Custom Made Prayers

This is how I start each day, but I add my own thoughts and prayers, such as "Help me be patient with ___________, give me understanding for ___________, and may I be a reflection of Your love to others."

~Linda N.

"The Lord has done it this very day; let us rejoice today and be glad."

Psalm 118:24

3 things I am thankful for today:

1.___________

2.___________

3.___________

What is one thing God wants me to do for Him today?

____

The Essence of Love

"Love is patient,
love is kind.
It does not envy,
it does not boast,
it is not proud."
1 Corinthians 13:4

This passage is often used at weddings, as it was at ours! It defines true love as a commitment to each other, seeking the best for our partner. It is a guide to our interactions with family, friends, and everyone that we encounter. How much better is life if we embrace this concept of love?

~Dotti K.

3 things I am thankful for today:

1.____________________

2.____________________

3.____________________

What is one thing God wants me to do for Him today?

We Owe Him Our Praises

God has provided for our salvation through His power and His mercy. He comes to our defense when we are attacked. He defeats the enemy and gives us a place of refuge. How can we withhold our praise? We should sing loud from the rooftops what a great and mighty God we have!

~Suzan R.

"But I will sing of thy power; yea, I will sing aloud of thy mercy in the morning: for thou hast been my defence and refuge in the day of my trouble."

Psalm 59:16 (KJV)

3 things I am thankful for today:

1.________________

2.________________

3.________________

What is one thing God wants me to do for Him today?

Trust the Timing

"'Be careful not to practice your righteousness in front of others to be seen by them. If you do, you will have no reward from your Father in heaven.'"

Matthew 6:1

God places good deeds in our heart so we feel this is something He wants us to do. No need to tell others about our generosity (trying to impress them to make us feel better). The reward will be in how we feel now, and God will reward us in His time.

~Tanya J.

3 things I am thankful for today:

1.________________________

2.________________________

3.________________________

What is one thing God wants me to do for Him today?

Banish Fear

God is with us. He has established a relationship with us and He assures us of His strength, help, and victory. Fear forgets God's promises, faithfulness, and power. It blinds our choices and makes trusting in God to provide the impossible. Our regular worship and spending time in the Word helps us remember what God desires and motivates us to obey Him more.

~Chris C.

"So do not fear, for I am with you; do not be dismayed, for I am your God. I will strengthen you and help you; I will uphold you with my righteous right hand."

Isaiah 41:10

3 things I am thankful for today:

1.____________________

2.____________________

3.____________________

What is one thing God wants me to do for Him today?

Gracefully Broken

"he saved us, not because of righteous things we had done, but because of his mercy. He saved us through the washing of rebirth and renewal by the Holy Spirit,"
Titus 3:5

The song *Gracefully Broken* is one of my favorites. I am so grateful to God that He gracefully broke my spirit from all the wrong in my life, so that now I stand here with my arms and my heart wide open, for God to multiply all I can be for Him.

~Peggy H.

3 things I am thankful for today:

1.____________________________

2.____________________________

3.____________________________

What is one thing God wants me to do for Him today?

Perfect Peace

A lot can disturb our peace as we get older. Will we age well? Do we have enough money? Will our spouse die? Will our friends die? Will we end up in a nursing home? God offers us a way to live out our older years in peace. How? Just set our mind on Him and keep it on Him! How? Open the Word and read His words to you. He alone offers perfect peace.

~Marilyn C.

"You will keep in perfect peace those whose minds are steadfast, because they trust in you."

Isaiah 26:3

3 things I am thankful for today:

1.____________________

2.____________________

3.____________________

What is one thing God wants me to do for Him today?

Knowing the Future Calms the Heart

"'Do not let your hearts be troubled. You believe in God; believe also in me. My Father's house has many rooms; if that were not so, would I have told you that I am going there to prepare a place for you? And if I go and prepare a place for you, I will come back and take you to be with me that you also may be where I am.'"

John 14:1-3

Potential anxious hearts stay calm when believing in God's authority over this troubled earth. Just as Jesus went back to Heaven to prepare a place for each one of God's children, we who believe Jesus are preparing ourselves for Jesus' return, to be taken to the Father's home, our forever glorious home in Heaven.

~Ruth N.

3 things I am thankful for today:

1.____________________

2.____________________

3.____________________

What is one thing God wants me to do for Him today?

Serve the Lord Always

We have a responsibility to share God's grace with members of our family. Once we have equipped our household, then we can go out and serve. From the firm foundation of a Christian home, we are prepared to let our light shine. Even as empty nesters with no grandchildren nearby, we can still let our light shine before a child or another adult.

~Steve B.

"'...But as for me and my household, we will serve the Lord.'"

Joshua 24:15

3 things I am thankful for today:

1.____________________

2.____________________

3.____________________

What is one thing God wants me to do for Him today?

Community Spirit

"He said to them, 'Then give back to Caesar what is Caesar's, and to God what is God's.'"
Luke 20:25

We do not ask to be delivered from dangers and burdens, but we do pray for wisdom and courage to speak truth to power. Help us to overcome our apathy. Strengthen us in our efforts to serve. May we be good citizens and true Christians in all things.

~Patty M.

3 things I am thankful for today:

1.____________________

2.____________________

3.____________________

What is one thing God wants me to do for Him today?

The Power of Prayer

God tells us to be bold in our prayers. We need to ask for what we want clearly, not bargaining or negotiating. We always need to pray for His will to be done, and for peace in the situation. God already knows our hearts and our needs, but He wants to hear from His children. What is on your heart today?

~Sharon B.

"'Ask and it will be given to you; seek and you will find; knock and the door will be opened to you.'"

Matthew 7:7

3 things I am thankful for today:

1.____________________

2.____________________

3.____________________

What is one thing God wants me to do for Him today?

Be Filled Again

"He asked me, 'Son of man, can these bones live?' I said, 'Sovereign Lord, you alone know.'"

Ezekiel 37:3

I am weary. I am tired. I hurt. And some days I simply feel defeated. Can these bones live? Dare to soak up the Word of God, to be filled again by the Spirit of God, and to let God work within these old bones that new life might spring forth! O Lord, You know my potential!

~Rev. Chris H.

3 things I am thankful for today:

1.____________________

2.____________________

3.____________________

What is one thing God wants me to do for Him today?

Living Without Labels

We often label ourselves by saying we are rich, poor, pretty, homely, fat, skinny, etc. But God tells us who we truly are to Him: we are His creation and handiwork. The only label we should ever use is CHOSEN.

~Jody M.

"For we are God's handiwork, created in Christ Jesus to do good works, which God prepared in advance for us to do."

Ephesians 2:10

3 things I am thankful for today:

1.____________________

2.____________________

3.____________________

What is one thing God wants me to do for Him today?

Who Would Worry?

"and that you may love the Lord your God, listen to his voice, and hold fast to him. For the Lord is your life, and he will give you many years in the land he swore to give to your fathers, Abraham, Isaac and Jacob."

Deuteronomy 30:20

Sometimes I feel God saying, "Stop worrying so you can hear my voice!" He is always close to us, but we hear other voices above His: doubt, confusion, worry. Be still and ask the Holy Spirit, our Comforter, to take away the world's noises so we can renew our minds with what God wants us to hear.

~Phillis R.

3 things I am thankful for today:

1.____________________

2.____________________

3.____________________

What is one thing God wants me to do for Him today?

Choose Joy!

If God saw the need to anoint Christ with the oil of joy, shouldn't we try to live joy-filled lives. According to Google, joy is to make peace with who you are, why you are, and how you are. Christ knew He was to be our Savior and, thankfully, came to peace with that. Let's strive to be joyful knowing that we can be saved by a joy-anointed Christ.

~Reba L.

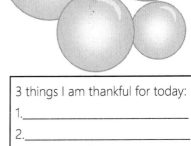

"'You have loved righteousness and hated wickedness; therefore God, your God, has set you above your companions by anointing you with the oil of joy.'"

Hebrews 1:9

3 things I am thankful for today:

1.__________

2.__________

3.__________

What is one thing God wants me to do for Him today?

Faith and Hope

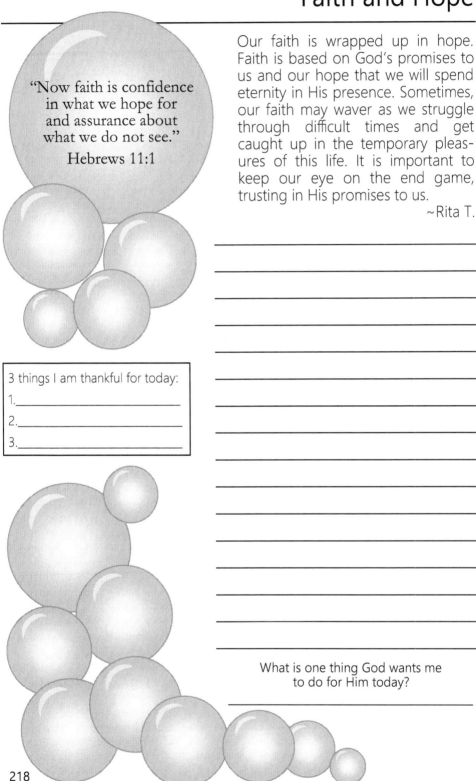

"Now faith is confidence in what we hope for and assurance about what we do not see."

Hebrews 11:1

Our faith is wrapped up in hope. Faith is based on God's promises to us and our hope that we will spend eternity in His presence. Sometimes, our faith may waver as we struggle through difficult times and get caught up in the temporary pleasures of this life. It is important to keep our eye on the end game, trusting in His promises to us.

~Rita T.

3 things I am thankful for today:

1.________________________

2.________________________

3.________________________

What is one thing God wants me to do for Him today?

Now What?

I was new in The Village – on my own, faced with some really big decisions after a life-changing event – a real deer in the headlights. But I wasn't alone – not really. Once I realized that, life shifted; a new path took shape. It's amazing how life can go on. Thank You, Lord.

~Susan M.

"When I said, 'My foot is slipping,' your unfailing love, Lord, supported me."

Psalm 94:18

3 things I am thankful for today:

1.____________________

2.____________________

3.____________________

What is one thing God wants me to do for Him today?

Authorities to Please

"The Pharisees, who loved money, heard all this and were sneering at Jesus. He said to them, "You are the ones who justify yourselves in the eyes of others, but God knows your hearts. What people value highly is detestable in God's sight."

Luke 16:14-15

Jesus warned the religious experts to reconsider whom they were trying to please, whose standards they were trying to meet, what their self-worth was built on. He warned them to evaluate their priorities. It is so easy to lose sight of the priorities in our lives that truly make us whole.

~Jim H.

3 things I am thankful for today:

1.________________________

2.________________________

3.________________________

What is one thing God wants me to do for Him today?

Lemonade, Anyone?

St. Paul's words make me think of making lemonade out of lemons. We encounter some very difficult circumstances in this village life as retirees, grandparents, or even parents; and we manage to do as Paul did by being content with what God has given us. We seem to bear our crosses with no pain.

~LunaGram

"...I have learned to be content whatever the circumstances."

Philippians 4:11

3 things I am thankful for today:

1.__________

2.__________

3.__________

What is one thing God wants me to do for Him today?

God Has Good Plans

"'For I know the plans I have for you,' declares the Lord, 'plans to prosper you and not to harm you, plans to give you hope and a future.'"

Jeremiah 29:11

This verse appeared in our 22-week *Walking with Purpose* Bible study program for modern women. Every time I read it (which is often because I made a poster of it for my home), I am filled with hope that God does indeed have good plans for me. I trust that, with God's help, I will fulfill those plans even when I encounter frustrations, confusion, or just fatigue.

~Paula D.

3 things I am thankful for today:

1.__________

2.__________

3.__________

What is one thing God wants me to do for Him today?

Know What Your Enemy Desires

Satan desires to separate us from God by controlling our emotions and spiritual thoughts. Any little discouragement can catch us off-guard, allowing Satan into our life. However, we're able to rule the wrestling match when we focus on praise and doing what's right in God's sight. God's power in us, is stronger than Satan's ability to hold us down.

~Ruth N.

"Then the Lord said to Cain, 'Why are you angry? Why is your face downcast? If you do what is right, will you not be accepted? But if you do not do what is right, sin is crouching at your door; it desires to have you, but you must rule over it.'"

Genesis 4:6-7

3 things I am thankful for today:

1.____________________

2.____________________

3.____________________

What is one thing God wants me to do for Him today?

Get Thee Behind Me, Satan!

"Be alert and of sober mind. Your enemy the devil prowls around like a roaring lion looking for someone to devour."

1 Peter 5:8

Someone once told me that Satan turns his warriors loose at 3:00AM. Have you ever felt him visit you about this time? I have! I awake to fear and panic, to confusion and feelings of insecurity. I begin praying and feel God's peace and love replace the negative feelings that awaken me. Blessed sleep follows.

~Vickie H.

3 things I am thankful for today:

1.____________________

2.____________________

3.____________________

What is one thing God wants me to do for Him today?

7. Planning for the Future

by Becky Mueller

My husband, Ken, and I had talked about death. In fact, his mother was dying. We were her caregivers. Little did we dream that death would come just after Ken turned 61!

We had just made major changes in our lives. After years in Bartlesville, Oklahoma, we decided to move to Hot Springs Village, where we had purchased a home years ago. We were in the middle of remodeling. Ken was quite the handyman, so he and I were doing much of the work ourselves.

And then the phone rang… Ken had died suddenly on Isabella Golf Course. He had been in the cart with one of his best friends. Word spreads quickly through Hot Springs Village, so I received a personal call to tell me the news.

Thank God for my NewComers Group. Although I missed several meetings, my fellow newcomers reached out to me with caring hearts, inviting me to events and get-togethers and, most of all, praying for me. I'm not sure I could have made it without them – I could feel their prayer covering.

Having been a Stephens Minister in Oklahoma, I now found myself on the receiving side of this ministry. In fact, I found myself joining support groups and going to church services and programs.

Much of my healing (I still have a long way to go) began as I started to pray for and help others. I know that you cannot pour from an empty vessel, but along with missing Ken, I felt the huge void of not doing what I had always done. So, through baby steps, I once again began minister to others in small ways.

What does God have in store for my future? If I've learned anything, it's that our plans are just *our plans*. God's plan may be entirely different, but I cling to His Promises and know that His Plan is Perfect! I pray daily, thanking God for my gift of faith and asking, "God, give me more faith every single day!" To quote a song I love, sung by Lea Ann Rimes, "There are things about tomorrow that I don't seem to understand, but I know who holds tomorrow and I know who holds my hand."*

> *"And this is the testimony: God has given us eternal life, and this life is in his Son. Whoever has the Son has life; whoever does not have the Son of God does not have life."* 1 John 5:11-12

> *"Why, you do not even know what will happen tomorrow. What is your life? You are a mist that appears for a little while and then vanishes."* James 4:14

**I Know Who Holds Tomorrow* written by Ira F Stanphill

Worry Not

As a wife and mother, so much of my time and efforts have revolved around shopping, cooking, cleaning, laundry, etc. Surely, God is not saying that I should let these things go—that God (or my husband?) would take care of it. The key point is that worry about these mundane issues can de-energize and defeat us. Another lesson in trust and priorities.

~Paula D.

"So do not worry, saying, 'What shall we eat?' or 'What shall we drink?' or 'What shall we wear?'... But seek first his kingdom and his righteousness, and all these things will be given to you as well."

Matthew 6:31,33

3 things I am thankful for today:

1.____________________

2.____________________

3.____________________

What is one thing God wants me to do for Him today?

Only One Way

"Jesus answered, 'I am the Way and the Truth and the Life. No one comes to the Father except through me.'"

John 14:6

Jesus came as God's salvation gift to the world. When Jesus told the disciples, His work was about finished, He was going back to heaven, the disciples had questions. Jesus clearly answered; "I am the Way and the Truth and the Life. No one comes to the Father except through me." You want to see God? Jesus is the way.

~Ruth N.

3 things I am thankful for today:

1.________________

2.________________

3.________________

What is one thing God wants me to do for Him today?

Patience is Required

Being patient is hard. After all, I have my "to do" list to accomplish. So, "God, please answer my prayers now." Well...that's not the way God works. I'm reminded to be patient, to wait for God's direction. He promises to hear my earnest requests. His plan, His "to do" list, is best; not mine.

~Debbie R.

"I waited patiently for the Lord; he turned to me and heard my cry."

Psalm 40:1

3 things I am thankful for today:

1.____________________

2.____________________

3.____________________

What is one thing God wants me to do for Him today?

Nothing But the Truth

"These are the things you are to do: Speak the truth to each other, and render true and sound judgment in your courts;..."
Zechariah 8:16

Imagine a world where every word uttered was true. Imagine all advertising was truthful and politicians spoke only true words. Imagine only truth being exchanged in our relationships. How differently would we live if we could only speak true words? Satan is the lover of lies, and lies are the cause of the heart-ache in this world. Let us strive to be the truth in this world.

~Sharon B.

3 things I am thankful for today:

1.____________________

2.____________________

3.____________________

What is one thing God wants me to do for Him today?

He Lifts Us

Have you had one of those days? Sure you have – we all do – and we carry the scars to prove it. Isaiah points us to the One who offers tender mercy and healing and strength for those hurting and in need. Jesus will not kick us while we're down; He will lift us up!

~Rev. Chris H.

"A bruised reed he will not break, and a smouldering wick he will not snuff out. In faithfulness he will bring forth justice."

Isaiah 42:3

3 things I am thankful for today:

1.__________________

2.__________________

3.__________________

What is one thing God wants me to do for Him today?

Pray Like This!

"This, then, is how you should pray:'Our Father in heaven, hallowed be your name, your kingdom come, your will be done, on earth as it is in heaven.'"

Matthew 6:9-10

It's so hard to know how to pray sometimes. Our needs can be overwhelming! When we don't know how to pray, when the needs are too great or too awful to consider, we can pray like this: "God, have Your way. Whatever that means, have Your way." He always answers this prayer, because His will is sure to be done.

~Marilyn C.

3 things I am thankful for today:

1.____________________

2.____________________

3.____________________

What is one thing God wants me to do for Him today?

____

How Long Does God's Love Last?

There's a Country & Western song that says, "And if love never lasts forever, then what's forever for?"* Like most things, what this world says is just the opposite of what God teaches. The phrase, "His love endures forever," is repeated 25 times In Psalm 136! How much clearer does God need to be?

~Vickie H.

"Give thanks to the Lord, for he is good. His love endures forever. Give thanks to the God of gods. His love endures forever."

Psalm 136:1-2

3 things I am thankful for today:

1.__________

2.__________

3.__________

What is one thing God wants me to do for Him today?

* *What's Forever For?* by Rafe Van Hoy; sung by Michael Martin Murphey

A Map for Your Lives

"There is a time
for everything,
and a season
for every activity
under the heavens."

Ecclesiastes 3:1

Sometimes our lives seem very complicated, and we get lost in the bustle of all our activities. We worry about the next "phase" of our life. But if we trust God and know He has a plan for us, we can survive anything and continue on our "path" in peace.

~Dotti K.

3 things I am thankful for today:

1.____________________

2.____________________

3.____________________

What is one thing God wants me to do for Him today?

Be Like a Child

When it comes to our faith, Jesus wants us to be like a child: full of wonderment, curiosity, and awe. Be as loving and trusting as a little child in God's word and you will be at peace and enjoy life more.

~Tanya J.

"But Jesus called the children to him and said, 'Let the little children come to me, and do not hinder them, for the kingdom of God belongs to such as these. Truly I tell you, anyone who will not receive the kingdom of God like a little child will never enter it.'"

Luke 18:16-17

3 things I am thankful for today:

1.____________________

2.____________________

3.____________________

What is one thing God wants me to do for Him today?

Be Still

"Jesus was in the stern, sleeping on a cushion. The disciples woke him and said to him, 'Teacher, don't you care if we drown?'"

Mark 4:38

How many times, when the storms and stresses of life hit, do we ask the question, "Don't You care?" Yet Jesus says, "Quiet! Be still!" to the storm then and today. When the storms come, lean into the power of God. He is our anchor. Don't underestimate His power to handle whatever storms that come our way.

~Chris C.

3 things I am thankful for today:

1.____________________

2.____________________

3.____________________

What is one thing God wants me to do for Him today?

The REAL Treasures

More, more, more... Do we need it? Folks in the Village love their weekly estate sales, but sometimes, the sales make me sad. All of those special treasures, accumulated over many years, now being picked over by strangers for pennies on the dollar. Let's give some thought to our REAL treasures – the love and promise of our Savior Jesus Christ.

~Susan M.

"I have learned the secret of being content in any and every situation, whether well fed or hungry, whether living in plenty or in want. I can do all this through him who gives me strength."

Philippians 4:12-13

3 things I am thankful for today:

1.____________________

2.____________________

3.____________________

What is one thing God wants me to do for Him today?

Anchor of Your Soul

"We have this hope as an anchor for the soul, firm and secure. It enters the inner sanctuary behind the curtain,"

Hebrews 6:19

What an anchor does depends on the length of the rope. With a short rope, the anchor would let the boat drift only a little way before the taut line tugged the boat back where it was supposed to be. My prayer is for me to keep God's anchor on a very short rope, always close to God's presence.

~Phillis R.

3 things I am thankful for today:

1.____________________

2.____________________

3.____________________

What is one thing God wants me to do for Him today?

Reservation is Made

I am glad that, as a 10-year-old boy, I trusted Christ as my Savior and was sealed with the Holy Spirit, which is the earnest (down payment) on my inheritance. 1 Peter 1:4 tells me that inheritance is incorruptible, undefiled, does not fade away and is reserved in heaven for me. My reservation is waiting for me.

~Steve R.

"In whom ye also trusted, after that ye heard the word of truth, the gospel of your salvation: in whom also after that ye believed, ye were sealed with that holy Spirit of promise,"

Ephesians 1:13 (KJV)

3 things I am thankful for today:

1.__________

2.__________

3.__________

What is one thing God wants me to do for Him today?

God is Light

"This is the message we have heard from him and declare to you: God is light; in him there is no darkness at all."

1 John 1:5

God is light. A bright light shows dust on the table, crumbs on the floor. Closed blinds and no lights doesn't allow you to know where you should clean: in your house and in your heart and life. I don't like the dark, period.

~Teela Y.

3 things I am thankful for today:

1.____________________

2.____________________

3.____________________

What is one thing God wants me to do for Him today?

Complete Control

In the Village, with curvy roads and no straight paths, it is often difficult to find our way or direction. When it comes to our life, we need to let God direct it 100%, not 40/60. It is comforting to know that He is in control and I don't need to worry! He has it figured out.

~LunaGram

"In all your ways submit to him, and he will make your paths straight."

Proverbs 3:6

3 things I am thankful for today:

1.________________________

2.________________________

3.________________________

What is one thing God wants me to do for Him today?

Express Your Feelings

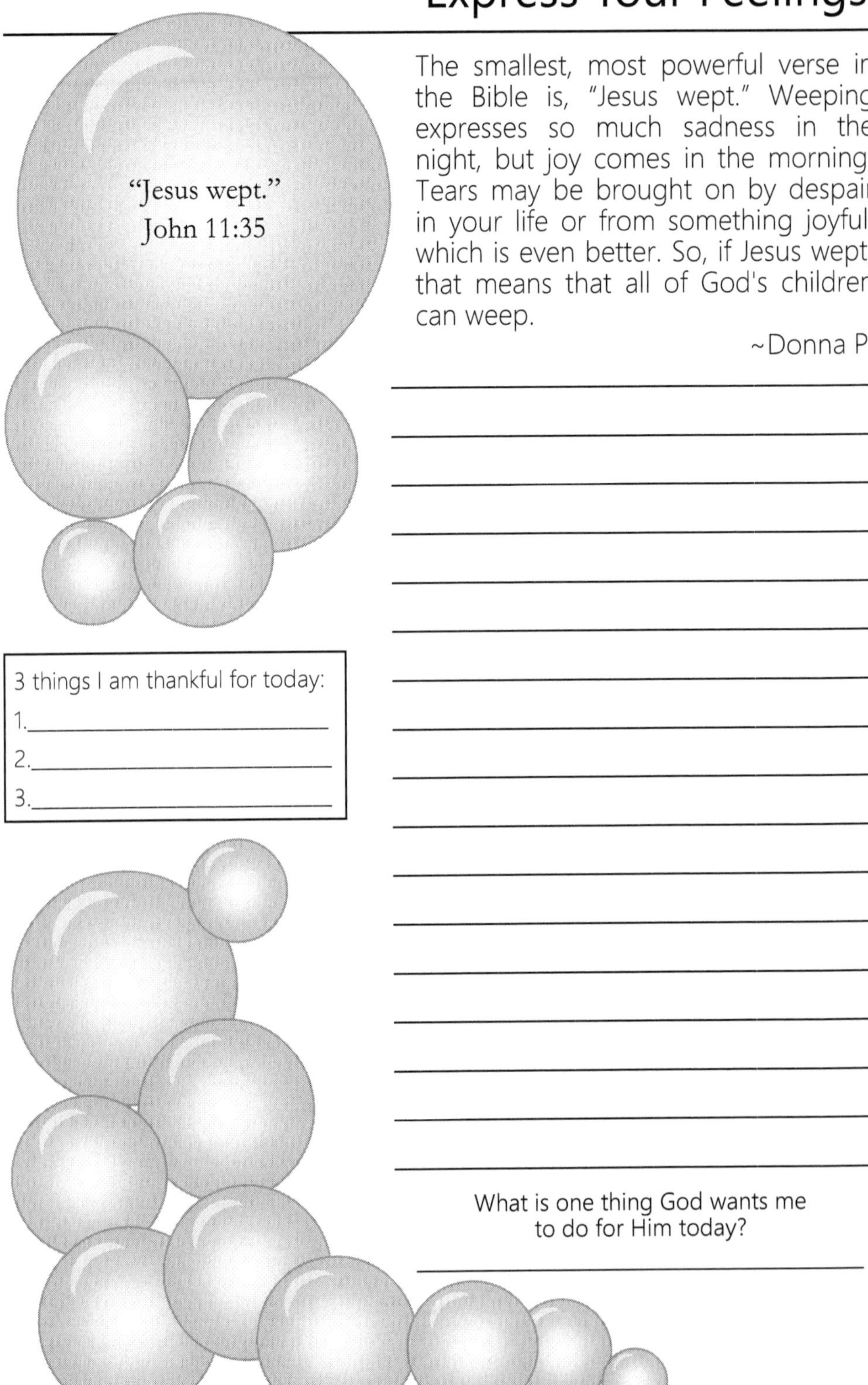

The smallest, most powerful verse in the Bible is, "Jesus wept." Weeping expresses so much sadness in the night, but joy comes in the morning. Tears may be brought on by despair in your life or from something joyful, which is even better. So, if Jesus wept, that means that all of God's children can weep.

~Donna P.

3 things I am thankful for today:

1.____________________

2.____________________

3.____________________

What is one thing God wants me to do for Him today?

Keep Eternity Values in View

A long span of emotional and/or physical suffering can be called a "heavy burden." However, Paul said we're using the wrong weight scale. When using God's heavenly balance scale, this earthly suffering is light compared with the weight of our Heavenly riches. Imagine our earthly dirty holey rags of sufferings becoming a heavenly purple robe lined with heavy precious jewels.

~Ruth N.

"For our light and momentary troubles are achieving for us an eternal glory that far outweighs them all."

2 Corinthians 4:17

3 things I am thankful for today:

1.____________________

2.____________________

3.____________________

What is one thing God wants me to do for Him today?

Knock, Knock. Who's There?

"Here I am! I stand at the door and knock. If anyone hears my voice and opens the door, I will come in and eat with that person, and they with me."

Revelation 3:20

Life in the Village can be overwhelmingly busy with golf, Pickleball, hiking, beaches, cards, etc. However, our Lord is waiting for us each day to open the door and let Him in to sit with us. He desires to give us the peace and joy of His Spirit. Knock, Knock. Will you answer the door?

~Jody M.

3 things I am thankful for today:

1.____________________

2.____________________

3.____________________

What is one thing God wants me to do for Him today?

A Good Name

Notice that the word here is CHOSEN. To choose to have a good name indicates that you come face-to-face with temptations, and choose rather to have a good name instead of ill-gotten riches. Satan tempted Jesus with riches, but Jesus rebuked him and chose the will of the Father. Make the eternal choice, not the temporal one. Heaven holds riches untold.

~Suzan R.

"A good name is rather to be chosen than great riches, and loving favour rather than silver and gold."
Proverbs 22:1 (KJV)

3 things I am thankful for today:

1.__________

2.__________

3.__________

What is one thing God wants me to do for Him today?

"So do not fear, for I am with you; do not be dismayed, for I am your God. I will strengthen you and help you; I will uphold you with my righteous right hand."

Isaiah 41:10

Years ago, a scary diagnosis and treatment plan became part of my everyday life. God's promise, and powerful prayer warrior intercession, enabled a calm can-do attitude during a difficult journey. When new challenges present themselves, I recall GLC – God's Loving Care, ALWAYS there.

~Chris S.

3 things I am thankful for today:

1.____________________

2.____________________

3.____________________

What is one thing God wants me to do for Him today?

Beginning and End

I hear You, Lord. It's not all about me. I am not the center of the universe. I am Your creation. You are my beginning and my end. You are my all in all. I give thanks, for I am Yours. Thanks be to God!

~Rev. Chris H.

"He said to me: 'It is done. I am the Alpha and the Omega, the Beginning and the End. To the thirsty I will give water without cost from the spring of the water of life. Those who are victorious will inherit all this, and I will be their God and they will be my children.'"

Revelation 21:6-7

3 things I am thankful for today:

1.____________________

2.____________________

3.____________________

What is one thing God wants me to do for Him today?

Expectant Prayer

"You did not choose me, but I chose you and appointed you so that you might go and bear fruit–fruit that will last–and so that whatever you ask in my name the Father will give you."

John 15:16

Whatever we ask in the Father's name...do we really believe it? Do we expect Him to answer us? Would we ignore our children? If they ask for something harmful or unfitting to the family name, yes. So, do we ask for things that will glorify our Lord? Are we known by the fruit we bear?

~Vickie H.

3 things I am thankful for today:

1.________________________

2.________________________

3.________________________

What is one thing God wants me to do for Him today?

Moans and Groans

Have there been times in your life when you were in so much pain that when you tried to pray, no words would do? Did your heart moan in grief? How comforting it is to know that the Spirit can pray for us and, without using words, asking the Father for exactly what we need.

~Diane G.

"In the same way, the Spirit helps us in our weakness. We do not know what we ought to pray for, but the Spirit himself intercedes for us through wordless groans."

Romans 8:26

____

____

____

____

____

____

____

____

____

____

____

____

____

____

____

____

____

3 things I am thankful for today:

1.______________________

2.______________________

3.______________________

What is one thing God wants me to do for Him today?

____

Freedom from Fear

"I sought the Lord,
and he answered me;
he delivered me
from all my fears."
Psalm 34:4

After a prolonged illness, I found I was looking at most events through a filter of fear. I was becoming more hesitant, less confident; worrying about situations that were not mine to influence. Now, when I tighten up and my mind starts to race, this verse re-directs my thoughts to the Lord who calms my fears.

~Sue K.

3 things I am thankful for today:

1.____________________

2.____________________

3.____________________

What is one thing God wants me to do for Him today?

God Is My Refuge

We know as Christians that our ultimate goal is eternal life in the presence of our God. So, as we face trials and tribulations on earth, we need to depend on our Lord to help us on our journey to our "forever" home.

~Dotti K.

"The Lord is my light and my salvation–whom shall I fear? The Lord is the stronghold of my life–of whom shall I be afraid?"

Psalm 27:1

3 things I am thankful for today:

1.__________

2.__________

3.__________

What is one thing God wants me to do for Him today?

Freedom in an Outstretched Arm

"Therefore, say to the Israelites: 'I am the Lord, and I will bring you out from under the yoke of the Egyptians. I will free you from being slaves to them, and I will redeem you with an outstretched arm and with mighty acts of judgment. I will take you as my own people, and I will be your God. Then you will know that I am the Lord your God, who brought you out from under the yoke of the Egyptians."

Exodus 6:6-7

The words "my outstretched arm" get me every time. That God looked out over the vast expanse of time and saw me, and then saw His son, with His outstretched arms nailed to a cross freeing me from the burden of sin...well, that is certainly a mighty act. And it was His plan from the very beginning.

~Kathy C.

3 things I am thankful for today:

1.__________

2.__________

3.__________

What is one thing God wants me to do for Him today?

Trusting God Equals Peace

As believers in the blood of Jesus Christ bringing our salvation, we also hold onto Jesus' promise of His peace. (John 14:27) Therefore, when we call out to Jesus, even in the middle of an emotional storm of grief, Jesus will guard our heart and mind from Satan's evil. Then we receive His peace that surpasses all understanding.

~Ruth N.

"And the peace of God, which transcends all understanding, will guard your hearts and your minds in Christ Jesus."

Philippians 4:7

3 things I am thankful for today:

1.____________________

2.____________________

3.____________________

What is one thing God wants me to do for Him today?

You Are Special

"But you are a chosen people, a royal priesthood, a holy nation, God's special possession, that you may declare the praises of him who called you out of darkness into his wonderful light."

1 Peter 2:9

Wow! We are God's special possessions. Each one of us—individually and collectively. We're special to our Almighty God. He chose us. He said, "I want you!" How can we fathom the greatness of that love? Take a moment and allow these thoughts to soak into your heart and soul. And then lift up praises to Him!

~Debbie R.

3 things I am thankful for today:

1.____________________

2.____________________

3.____________________

What is one thing God wants me to do for Him today?

No Answers Yet

God's expression of His unconditional love is found throughout the Bible. Although we are commanded to repent our sins and strive towards the way of God, He never stops loving us in our journey to righteousness. The Bible shows us that God's unconditional love never fails.

~Peggy H.

"And so we know and rely on the love God has for us. God is love. Whoever lives in love lives in God, and God in them."

1 John 4:16

3 things I am thankful for today:

1.__________

2.__________

3.__________

What is one thing God wants me to do for Him today?

We Are on a Journey

"Surely your goodness and love will follow me all the days of my life, and I will dwell in the house of the Lord forever."

Psalm 23:6

We're not home yet! We have our suitcases packed and ready, as we go from place to place, through all that God has for us here. But we haven't reached our destination! Surely, His goodness and love follows us all the way. The day will come when we get to the house of the Lord. The journey will be over, and we'll unpack those suitcases and stay forever. But not yet.

~Marilyn C

____

____

____

____

____

____

____

____

____

____

____

____

____

____

____

3 things I am thankful for today:

1.______________________________

2.______________________________

3.______________________________

What is one thing God wants me to do for Him today?

____

Good Guys Finish Best

Often, the wicked do prosper, at least for a while, adding to the temptation to prosper with them. We still need to keep doing "the next right thing." We may or may not see them get their "just rewards." The wicked remove themselves from God's presence, a punishment in itself. The peace we receive from not straying off the right path trumps ill-gotten gains.

~Sharon B.

"For the Lord watches over the way of the righteous, but the way of the wicked leads to destruction."

Psalms 1:6

3 things I am thankful for today:

1.____________

2.____________

3.____________

What is one thing God wants me to do for Him today?

8. What if God Mystery Shopped You?

by Vickie Henry

I was blessed to own one of the first Mystery Shopping companies in the world, Feedback Plus. In 1983, many people had no idea what mystery shopping was, but I was excited about the concept from day one.

With nearly 500,000 mystery shoppers across the country, we would telephone or go into retail stores, restaurants, and banks to pose as customers and interact with employees. We would evaluate customer service by seeing whether employees were friendly, knowledgeable, and using good sales skills. Our clients, such as Neiman Marcus, Crate and Barrel, El Chico, First City Banks, and hundreds of others, could find out how their employees treated customers.

As CEO of Feedback Plus for 30+ years, I was asked to present the results of our mystery shopping visits. My presentation was entitled *Would You Do Business With YOU?* and it led to a very lucrative public speaking career for me.

Now that I'm retired, I have adapted this seminar for faith-based audiences, and have given it the title *What if God Mystery Shopped YOU?* The 10-point questionnaire is nearly the same as the one we used for generic telephone mystery shops. The difference is that instead of mystery shoppers calling clients, we pretend that God is calling us!

So, imagine that you are receiving a call from God right now…

1. How many times would the phone ring?
2. Would you be pleasant and friendly?
3. Would you put God on hold?
4. Are you really interested in what He has to say?
5. Do you have good product knowledge?
6. Would you be able to help Him?
7. At any time, would your demeanor change?
8. Would you say, "Thank You?"
9. Based on this one call, will God call on you again?
10. And, based on this one call, would you recommend God to a friend?

As you can see, sometimes how we react to other callers can also be a reflection of our approach to God.

When you see God on your caller-ID, you may be honored; however, you may let the phone ring a few times, hesitating because your day is full of your own plans. You really don't want them to be disrupted.

If a friend calls, you may be tempted to put God on hold.

> Product knowledge is a good one – Do you read your Bible? God has given us a handbook!

Will you say "Yes!" to God?

> Do you thank Him for all things?

Do you think He'll call you again?

> Would you tell others about God? To many lost souls, you may be the only Jesus they see today!

If you find this concept appealing, it would be an honor for me to speak to your church group or Christian organization.

> *"...From everyone who has been given much, much will be demanded, and from the one who has been entrusted with much, much more will be asked."*
> Luke 12:48

Are You One of His Heirs?

Just consider for a moment: God made a promise to Abraham that his seed, generation after generation forever onwards would be heirs to His kingdom. Then, because of Jesus' sacrifice on the Cross, when His blood washed away our sins, we now receive our inheritance through the gift of God's grace rather than having to earn it with good works...but only if we belong to Christ!

~Warren W.

"If you belong to Christ, then you are Abraham's seed, and heirs according to the promise."

Galatians 3:29

3 things I am thankful for today:

1.____________________

2.____________________

3.____________________

What is one thing God wants me to do for Him today?

FEAR=False Evidence Appearing Real

"For the Spirit God gave us does not make us timid, but gives us power, love and self-discipline."

2 Timothy 1:7

What do you fear? I'm afraid of bridges, high places and even carnival rides. I know that false evidence does not have power over me, and I pray often, "Fear does not have power over me, in the name of God who gives me the power to overcome all things!" I've experienced many losses, but I'll never give up on myself and God. We're a team!

~Phillis R.

3 things I am thankful for today:

1.____________________

2.____________________

3.____________________

What is one thing God wants me to do for Him today?

Hold That Tongue

I should have bought a t-shirt with a saying on the front that reads "I am a good person, but oh that mouth!" Do you find yourself regretting something you are saying, even as it leaves your mouth? We create our world by the words we speak. What type of world have you been creating for yourself?

~Diane G.

"My dear brothers and sisters, take note of this: Everyone should be quick to listen, slow to speak and slow to become angry,"

James 1:19

3 things I am thankful for today:

1.____________________

2.____________________

3.____________________

What is one thing God wants me to do for Him today?

Peace at Last!

"Come to me, all you who are weary and burdened, and I will give you rest."

Matthew 11:28

I want to put an exclamation point at the end of this verse and quote it every day. Oftentimes, I feel weary and burdened and wonder if I will make it to the next day. Although the verse itself is not about the everyday weariness of life, but about the ultimate finality of Peace in Heaven, Jesus knows where I am coming from!

~LunaGram

3 things I am thankful for today:

1.____________________

2.____________________

3.____________________

What is one thing God wants me to do for Him today?

Be an Overcomer

Trouble comes when we least expect it. And it comes in many forms – war, illness, death of a loved one, failed relationships, loss of a job. Sometimes when we feel like we're doing everything right, the enemy attacks. Jesus reminds us that He has overcome the world for us.

~Steve B.

"I have told you these things, so that in me you may have peace. In this world you will have trouble. But take heart! I have overcome the world."

John 16:33

3 things I am thankful for today:

1.__________

2.__________

3.__________

What is one thing God wants me to do for Him today?

Comparing Wise and Foolish

"Through desire a man, having separated himself, seeketh and intermeddleth with all wisdom. A fool hath no delight in understanding, but that his heart may discover itself."

Proverbs 18:1-2 (KJV)

Verse 1 shows a man that has a desire to be wise. He spends time immersing himself in God's word, searching for wisdom. Christians should desire to commune with God and learn His wisdom to use in everyday life.

Verse 2 shows a person who cares only about what today's vocabulary calls "finding himself." The Bible calls him a fool. Christians should be careful not to get sucked into this philosophy.

~Suzan R.

3 things I am thankful for today:

1.____________________

2.____________________

3.____________________

What is one thing God wants me to do for Him today?

Am I Really Loving?

Love requires action. What am I doing intentionally to show my love to God? Am I following His commandments? How do I show love to others? Take practical steps to show you truly love.

~Betty W.

"Jesus replied: 'Love the Lord your God with all your heart and with all your soul and with all your mind.' This is the first and greatest commandment. And the second is like it: 'Love your neighbor as yourself.'"

Matthew 22:37-39

3 things I am thankful for today:

1.__________

2.__________

3.__________

What is one thing God wants me to do for Him today?

Old Age

"Listen to your father, who gave you life, and do not despise your mother when she is old."

Proverbs 23:22

I moved to the Hot Springs area to take care of my mother. As she has slowed down and experienced more memory problems, it becomes more of a challenge to deal with her. This verse keeps me in the correct frame of mind.

~Julie K

3 things I am thankful for today:

1.____________________

2.____________________

3.____________________

What is one thing God wants me to do for Him today?

Time Passages

Most Villagers can too easily identify with the words from the song *Time Passages,** "The years run too short and the days too fast." God entreats us to use our days wisely, understanding that we will feel there will be far too few in our time on earth.

~Rita T.

"Teach us to number our days, that we may gain a heart of wisdom."

Psalm 90:12

3 things I am thankful for today:

1.____________________

2.____________________

3.____________________

What is one thing God wants me to do for Him today?

* *Time Passages* by Al Stewart

Your Yoke Is Easy?

"For my yoke is easy and my burden is light."
Matthew 11:30

I must admit, sometimes the yoke is heavy and even painful. It isn't always easy to be a true Christian...to do what I think Jesus asks or expects...but that's because I'm self-centered and try to "do it all" myself. I need to surrender and trust God to give me the strength and wisdom to overcome my innate selfishness, weaknesses, and faults.

~Paula D.

3 things I am thankful for today:

1.____________________

2.____________________

3.____________________

What is one thing God wants me to do for Him today?

God Rocks

I love rocks! God's beauty resides in every rock I find. I'm always looking down when I'm near rocks, seeking rocks with "crosses" in the grain, heart shaped rocks, or odd shaped rocks I can paint into something clever. Many I paint, then add a bible verse and leave somewhere to be discovered. I love sharing my God Rocks.

~Vicki F.

"You will seek me and find me when you seek me with all your heart."

Jeremiah 29:13

3 things I am thankful for today:

1.__________

2.__________

3.__________

What is one thing God wants me to do for Him today?

Now, THAT'S the Spirit!

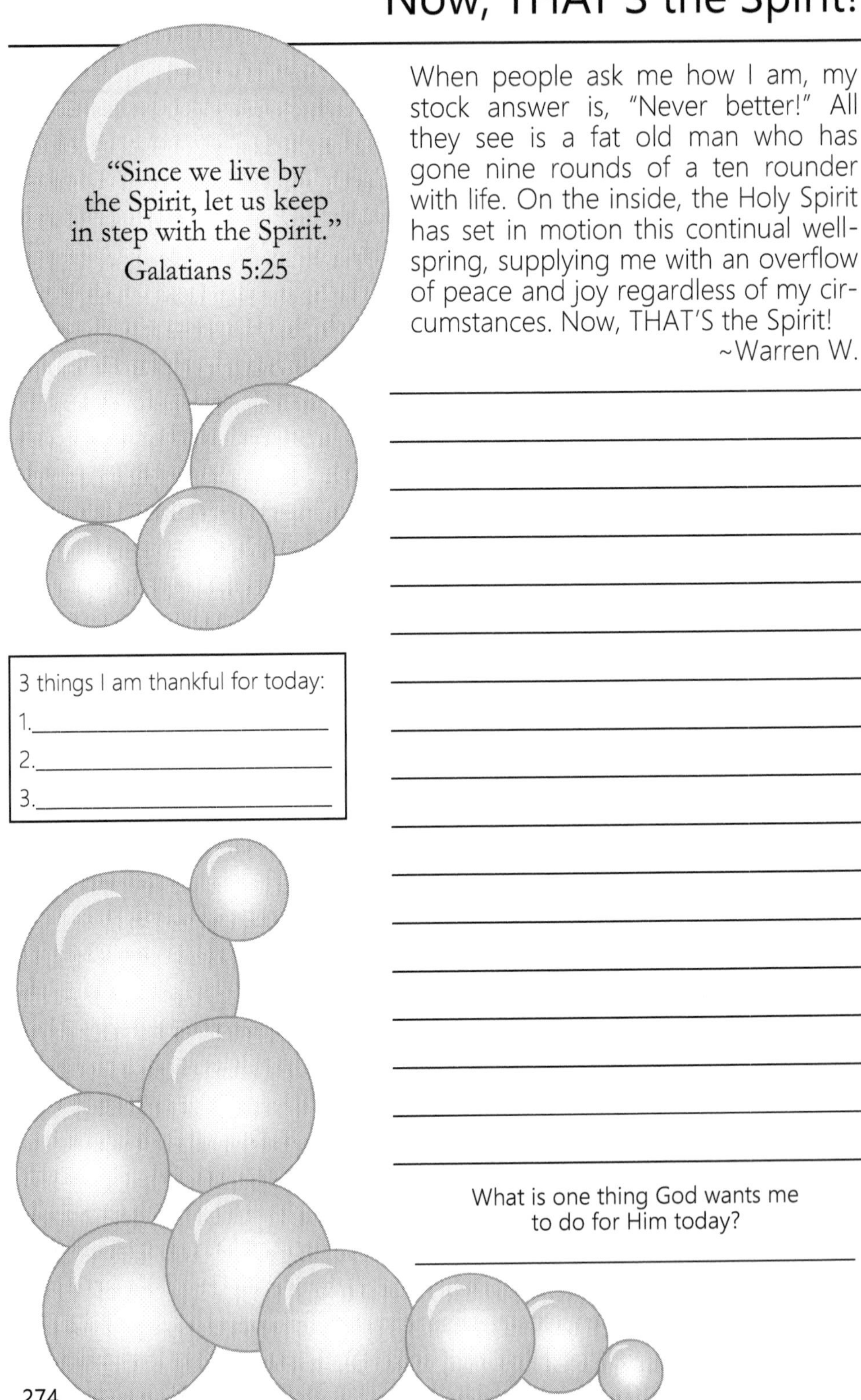

"Since we live by
the Spirit, let us keep
in step with the Spirit."
Galatians 5:25

When people ask me how I am, my stock answer is, "Never better!" All they see is a fat old man who has gone nine rounds of a ten rounder with life. On the inside, the Holy Spirit has set in motion this continual well-spring, supplying me with an overflow of peace and joy regardless of my circumstances. Now, THAT'S the Spirit!

~Warren W.

3 things I am thankful for today:

1.____________________

2.____________________

3.____________________

What is one thing God wants me to do for Him today?

Christian Communication

Good, effective communication takes work. How often do misunderstandings arise because we're too focused on what we want to say, instead of actually listening to what others are saying? Let's follow Jesus' example: He often demonstrated the importance of both caring and listening. Slow down, listen, ask questions. Anger can often be avoided.

~Susan M.

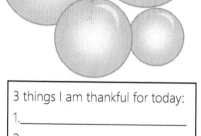

"My dear brothers and sisters, take note of this: Everyone should be quick to listen, slow to speak and slow to become angry,"

James 1:19

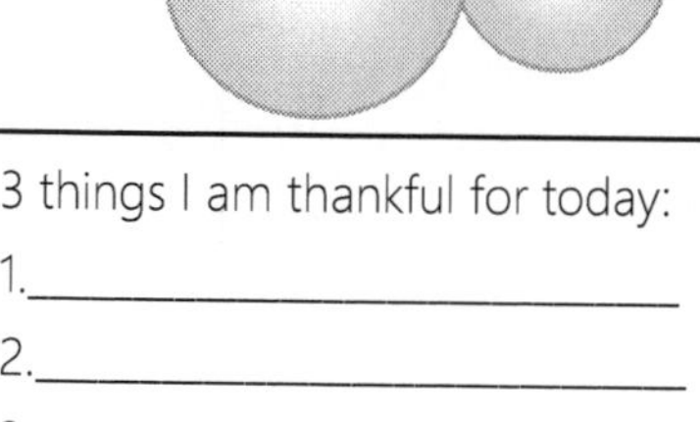

3 things I am thankful for today:

1.____________________

2.____________________

3.____________________

What is one thing God wants me to do for Him today?

Let Us Be Merciful

"The Lord has heard my cry for mercy; the Lord accepts my prayer."

Psalm 6:9

When you feel wronged by someone, are you able to forgive them and show them mercy? When we falter, the Lord is always ready to forgive us and shower His mercy upon us! Our world would be a more peaceful place if we could all imitate the Lord in this way.

~Dotti K.

3 things I am thankful for today:

1.____________________

2.____________________

3.____________________

What is one thing God wants me to do for Him today?

Answer the Question

Many people never face the question. Many confronted with the question evade answering it. Many change their answer over time. The fundamental claim of the Christian faith is Jesus Christ, or more clearly, "Jesus is the Christ." We can respond with a "So what?" shrug, an "I don't know that," or an "I'm in, whatever it takes." Daily.

~Jim H.

"Once when Jesus was praying in private and his disciples were with him, he asked them, 'Who do the crowds say I am? …But what about you?' he asked. 'Who do you say I am?' Peter answered, 'God's Messiah.'"

Luke 9:18,20

3 things I am thankful for today:

1.________________

2.________________

3.________________

What is one thing God wants me to do for Him today?

Change the World

"...but thou art a God ready to pardon, gracious and merciful, slow to anger, and of great kindness, and forsookest them not."

Nehemiah 9:17 (KJV)

It is great to know that this is the kind of God we serve. The Bible tells us to strive to be like God. Gandhi said, "If it weren't for Christians, I'd be a Christian." Maybe we should all strive to be better Christians and influence those around us for Christ.

~Steve R.

3 things I am thankful for today:

1.________________

2.________________

3.________________

What is one thing God wants me to do for Him today?

An Encouraging Word

Have you had a bad day, then had your spirits uplifted by a smile or kind word? God bless those people! Let's not keep small words or acts of kindness merely in our thoughts. Consider how that cranky cashier with lovely eyes might treasure a compliment during an exhausting shift!

~Chris S.

"Light in a messenger's eyes brings joy to the heart, and good news gives health to the bones."

Proverbs 15:30

3 things I am thankful for today:

1.__________

2.__________

3.__________

What is one thing God wants me to do for Him today?

The Perfect Plan

"For we are God's handiwork, created in Christ Jesus to do good works, which God prepared in advance for us to do."

Ephesians 2:10

God laid out a good plan for us before we were born to include health, happiness, and fulfilment. Study His word to seek direction. But also remember that Satan strives to disrupt this plan and we will have our own trials to overcome with God's help.

~Tanya J.

3 things I am thankful for today:

1.____________________

2.____________________

3.____________________

What is one thing God wants me to do for Him today?

Jesus Paid It All

"'Cause Jesus paid it all. All to Him I owe. Sin had left a crimson stain, He washed it white as snow."* I don't know about you, but the older I get, the more I realize just how much sin has stained my life, how much I have done that is NOT God-honoring. To know I am washed clean, completely clean, is my greatest blessing.

~Marilyn C.

"Therefore, there is now no condemnation for those who are in Christ Jesus."
Romans 8:1

3 things I am thankful for today:

1.____________________

2.____________________

3.____________________

What is one thing God wants me to do for Him today?

* *Jesus Paid It All* by Kristian Stanfill

Do You Have a Barcelona?

"Have I not commanded you? Be strong and courageous. Do not be afraid; do not be discouraged, for the Lord your God will be with you wherever you go."

Joshua 1:9

It seems so funny now, but several years ago I got lost on Barcelona Road here in the Village. Yes, that straight-a-way road Barcelona. I literally handed God the steering wheel to my car and my life. It's in the stressful times that we grow closer to Him.

~Peggy H.

3 things I am thankful for today:

1.____________________

2.____________________

3.____________________

What is one thing God wants me to do for Him today?

The Heart of the Matter

So many times, since becoming a Christian, I have thought, "O, God, I am so thankful You know my heart." and following that, "O, God, I am so sorry You know my heart." May we all seek to say, think and do the things that reflect Christ and honors God.

~Reba L.

"As water reflects a face, so one's life reflects the heart."

Proverbs 27:19

3 things I am thankful for today:

1.____________________

2.____________________

3.____________________

What is one thing God wants me to do for Him today?

Bumps in the Road

"And we know that in all things God works for the good of those who love him, who have been called according to his purpose."

Romans 8:28

Father, may we have a living faith in Thee which will enable us not only to endure injuries, illnesses, and disappointments, but to reform them into learning moments. Our prayer is not that You take the irritating conditions from us, but that we will learn all we need from them.

~Patty M.

3 things I am thankful for today:

1.________________________

2.________________________

3.________________________

What is one thing God wants me to do for Him today?

Spiritual Fitness

Today there is much emphasis placed on physical fitness and training. But what about our spiritual fitness? Strong faith comes from hearing and reading God's Word. Let us be diligent in consistently training our spiritual muscles to gain a strong faith.

~Chris C.

"Have nothing to do with godless myths and old wives' tales; rather, train yourself to be godly."

1 Timothy 4:7

3 things I am thankful for today:

1.____________________

2.____________________

3.____________________

What is one thing God wants me to do for Him today?

Chin Up!

"Have I not commanded you? Be strong and courageous. Do not be afraid; do not be discouraged, for the Lord your God will be with you wherever you go."
Joshua 1:9

How quickly we forget that God is with us always. When we walk through the dark, we can hold our heads up high. Be it the frustration we experience with our children or grandchildren, or perhaps illness, financial crisis, or loss of a loved one; we can always turn to our loving God in Prayer and He will see us through.
~LunaGram

3 things I am thankful for today:
1.________________________
2.________________________
3.________________________

What is one thing God wants me to do for Him today?

Doers of the Word

We know that doing good works or being a good person is not in the formula for salvation. James admonishes us to be "doers of the word and not hearers only." True faith is manifested in how we live our lives. The popular rubber bracelet WWJD (what would Jesus do?) is the question we should ponder before our decision-making is complete.

~Diane G.

"Do not merely listen to the word, and so deceive yourselves. Do what is says."

James 1:22

____

____

____

____

____

____

____

____

____

____

____

____

____

____

____

____

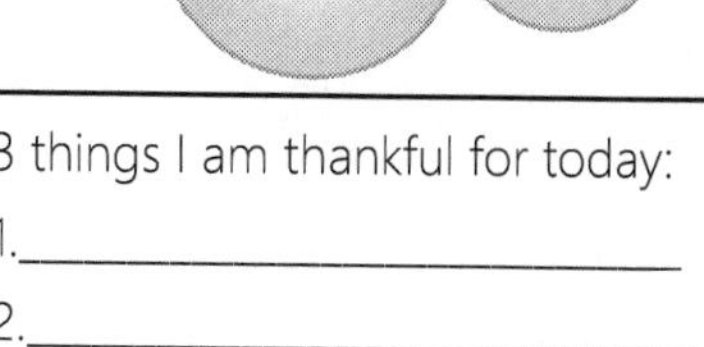

3 things I am thankful for today:

1.____________________

2.____________________

3.____________________

What is one thing God wants me to do for Him today?

____

Rejoice and Be Glad

"The Lord has done it this very day; let us rejoice today and be glad."

Psalm 118:24

On days when I get up "on the wrong side of the bed," this verse helps me to adjust my perspective. God has made this day. He is allowing me to be in it. He has blessed me with another day to live for Him. How could I not rejoice and be glad? God is good, all the time!

~Debbie R.

3 things I am thankful for today:

1.____________________

2.____________________

3.____________________

What is one thing God wants me to do for Him today?

How Can You Say Anything Wrong?

Do you fear public speaking? Or are you facing a difficult conversation with one of your children, your spouse, or a friend? Pray; ask God to take over! What He did for Paul in prison, He will do for you! You will feel the Holy Spirit speaking through you, whether you are speaking to 100 or one.

~Vickie H.

"But when they arrest you, do not worry about what to say or how to say it. At that time you will be given what to say, for it will not be you speaking, but the Spirit of your Father speaking through you."

Matthew 10:19-20

3 things I am thankful for today:

1.____________________

2.____________________

3.____________________

What is one thing God wants me to do for Him today?

What Am I Wearing Today?

"Therefore, as God's chosen people, holy and dearly loved, clothe yourselves with compassion, kindness, humility, gentleness and patience."

Colossians 3:12

We should not clothe ourselves with attitudes we quickly put on and take off as we choose. Compassion, kindness, humility, gentleness, and patience are preplanned attitudes to be put on each morning in the dressing room of our heart. Wear only attitudes with the "Designed by God" label.

~Ruth N.

3 things I am thankful for today:

1.____________________

2.____________________

3.____________________

What is one thing God wants me to do for Him today?

Watch What You Say

The world has enough critics; be an encourager instead. Cultivate the habit of complimenting someone daily. Be generous with your gratitude and praise. My agency moved from shabby quarters into a beautiful new building and change-resisters loudly complained. A co-worker and I privately decided to counter each negative with three positives, and we watched the atmosphere change. Encouragement is contagious!

~Sharon B.

"Do not let any unwholesome talk come out of your mouths, but only what is helpful for building others up according to their needs, that it may benefit those who listen."

Ephesians 4:29

3 things I am thankful for today:

1.__________

2.__________

3.__________

What is one thing God wants me to do for Him today?

Our Plans May Land Us in Mud

"Command those who are rich in this present world not to be arrogant nor to put their hope in wealth, which is so uncertain, but to put their hope in God, who richly provides us with everything for our enjoyment."

1 Timothy 6:17

Have you ever charged forward with your plans, not giving a thought to whether they are part of God's perfect plan for you? I have. Then, when we muddle around, usually trying to undo some of our plans. We finally fall to our knees and say, "God! Help me!" How much better to do this process.

~Phillis R.

3 things I am thankful for today:

1.____________________

2.____________________

3.____________________

What is one thing God wants me to do for Him today?

The Power of Proper Praying

Prayer is an earnest conversation between us and God. We pray, He listens. But when He speaks, we better do the listening. When we ask Him for something, it better be for something that will be for the greater good – something that will be a reflection of His glory. A new car may not be in God's plans.

~Warren W.

"And I will do whatever you ask in my name, so that the Father may be glorified in the Son."

John 14:13

3 things I am thankful for today:

1.____________________

2.____________________

3.____________________

What is one thing God wants me to do for Him today?

9. Forgiving the Unforgivable

by Kathy Sanders

Kathy Sanders' life was changed forever when a bomb destroyed the Alfred P. Murrah Federal Building in Oklahoma City, Oklahoma, killing her two grandsons, Chase and Colton.

For months, Kathy struggled to cope with the terrible loss of her grandsons and wondered if the God she had worshipped all of her life even existed. After battling bitterness and contemplating suicide, she turned to the Lord and asked what He would have her do. The answer was clear: Forgive your enemies.

Thus, Kathy began a tentative friendship with the mother of Terry Nichols, one of the men convicted of the bombing. Over time, that friendship extended to Nichols himself via phone conversations, letters, and even face-to-face meetings.

While searching for answers about what happened that fateful day in April, Kathy found opportunities to cultivate relationships with Nichols's children, sister, wife, and ex-wife in separate turns. Kathy demonstrated the same type of warmth to family members of Timothy McVeigh, the second man convicted of orchestrating the bombing. Her courageous efforts of extending compassion and grace gave her peace and removed the bitterness from her life.

Kathy shared her story of walking the road less traveled in her book Now You See Me, How I Forgave the Unforgiveable, including photos, interviews, and actual letters exchanged with Terry Nichols. Her next book, due to be released in 2020, will cover her findings from 25 years of research and reveal what she feels really happened on April 19, 1995. Kathy looks forward to more opportunities to spread God's goodness and emphasize His teachings of forgiveness.

Today, Kathy and her husband are proud residents of Hot Springs Village, Arkansas. They have six children and 15 grandchildren (including Chase and Colton who are waiting in Heaven). As a painter, she uses her art to capture life's important moments and touch peoples' lives. She is also in high demand as a speaker.

> *"'And forgive your people, who have sinned against you; forgive all the offenses they have committed against you, and cause their captors to show them mercy;'"* 1 Kings 8:50
>
> *"And forgive us our debts, as we also have forgiven our debtors."* Matthew 6:12
>
> *"For in the same way you judge others, you will be judged, and with the measure you use, it will be measured to you."* Matthew 7:2

Resilience

Why do some people bounce back from hardships and others don't? Job had a multitude of challenges, yet his "latter days were more (blessed) than his beginnings." God's wrath towards Job's rebuking friends required Job to pray for those friends, unlocking bountiful blessings for Job. Likewise, we must pray for offending circumstances and people, so we too can bounce back from hurt to blessings.

~Sharon B.

"After Job had prayed for his friends, the Lord restored his fortunes and gave him twice as much as he had before."

Job 42:10

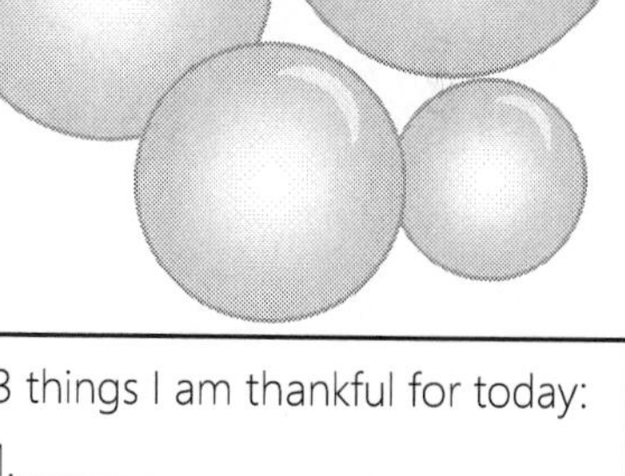

3 things I am thankful for today:

1.__________________

2.__________________

3.__________________

What is one thing God wants me to do for Him today?

Praying for a Prodigal

"I will give you a new heart and put a new spirit in you; I will remove from you your heart of stone and give you a heart of flesh. And I will put my Spirit in you and move you to follow my decrees and be careful to keep my laws."

Ezekiel 36:26-27

When tears flow and the stomach aches, yet no words come while trying to pray for a prodigal family member or friend, turn to Scripture. Read God's words back to Him. Stand in faith, believing God will do what He said He would do. "Lord remove (name)'s heart of stone, put Your Spirit in (name), all for Your glory and praise."

~Ruth N.

3 things I am thankful for today:

1.________________

2.________________

3.________________

What is one thing God wants me to do for Him today?

Looking Forward

The Bible doesn't promise us an easy life; we'll have troubles of all types. But we can be assured that our troubles will be used in some way to God's glory. And when we contemplate how incredibly glorious eternity with God will be, our troubles today will seem light and momentary in comparison. Let's look forward.

~Debbie R.

"For our light and momentary troubles are achieving for us an eternal glory that far outweighs them all."

2 Corinthians 4:17

3 things I am thankful for today:

1.___________________________

2.___________________________

3.___________________________

What is one thing God wants me to do for Him today?

Walk On

"Even though I walk through the darkest valley, I will fear no evil, for you are with me; your rod and your staff, they comfort me."

Psalm 23:4

Knowing God personally requires trusting Him through hard times. Be faithful, do whatever He says, be steadfast while waiting for Him to work out our problems. God is understanding, faithful, and good in His deliverance in your life. Your faith increases by going through tough times. Don't run away from God; draw near to Him and listen for His voice of assurance.

~Peggy H.

3 things I am thankful for today:

1.____________________

2.____________________

3.____________________

What is one thing God wants me to do for Him today?

A Cross Walk With Me

We carefully planned every detail when building our new home in Hot Springs Village. It was built and established in 2005. Bible verses are under our foundation, inside the walls, and on the walls. Every room has a cross hanging on a wall. Our grand-children love to take a "cross walk" with me when they come to visit us.

~Vicki F.

"By wisdom a house is built, and through understanding it is established; through knowledge its rooms are filled with rare and beautiful treasures."

Proverb 24:3-4

3 things I am thankful for today:

1.__________

2.__________

3.__________

What is one thing God wants me to do for Him today?

The Lord's Giveaway

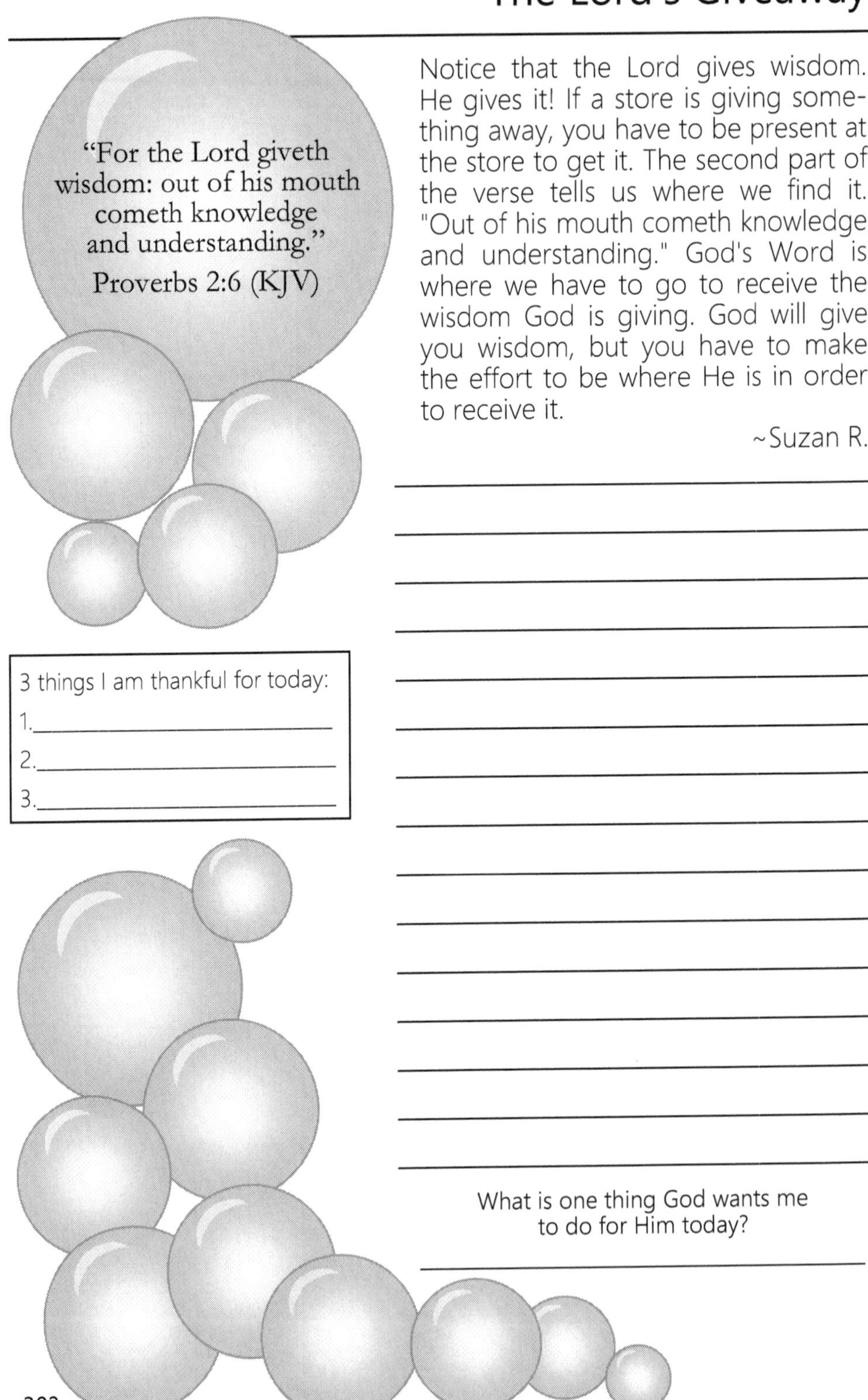

"For the Lord giveth wisdom: out of his mouth cometh knowledge and understanding."
Proverbs 2:6 (KJV)

Notice that the Lord gives wisdom. He gives it! If a store is giving something away, you have to be present at the store to get it. The second part of the verse tells us where we find it. "Out of his mouth cometh knowledge and understanding." God's Word is where we have to go to receive the wisdom God is giving. God will give you wisdom, but you have to make the effort to be where He is in order to receive it.

~Suzan R.

3 things I am thankful for today:

1.____________________

2.____________________

3.____________________

What is one thing God wants me to do for Him today?

His Will, Not Mine

How many times a day do we tell ourselves, "I've got this," when in reality, "God's got this." God has you in His hands and everlasting love. If only we would trust Him and go to Him first...

~Linda N.

"Praise be to the Lord, to God our Savior, who daily bears our burdens."

Psalm 68:19

3 things I am thankful for today:

1.____________________

2.____________________

3.____________________

What is one thing God wants me to do for Him today?

Forgive as We are Forgiven

"For if you forgive other people when they sin against you, your heavenly Father will also forgive you. But if you do not forgive others their sins, your Father will not forgive your sins."

Matthew 6:14-15

Immediately following the teaching of the Lord's Prayer, this passage reminds us that we should forgive others as we would want forgiveness for ourselves. At its heart, it's a variation of the Golden Rule – "Do unto others..."

~Ike E.

3 things I am thankful for today:

1.____________________

2.____________________

3.____________________

What is one thing God wants me to do for Him today?

He Will Tell Us Everything

Wouldn't it be wonderful if Jesus spoke to us so clearly and directly? Instead, my own conscience wrestles with my personal desires as I try to discern certain meanings and actions – to figure out just what I should think or do. Yet directives are clear: Love God and your neighbor as yourself. LOVE.

~Paula D.

"The woman said, 'I know that Messiah' (called Christ) 'is coming. When he comes, he will explain everything to us.' Then Jesus declared, 'I, the one speaking to you–I am he.'"

John 4:25-26

3 things I am thankful for today:

1.________________

2.________________

3.________________

What is one thing God wants me to do for Him today?

Music to Our Ears

"Come, let us sing for joy to the Lord; let us shout aloud to the Rock of our salvation. Let us come before him with thanksgiving and extol him with music and song."

Psalms 95:1-2

Music, the universal language, is refreshing, uplifting, and just makes you feel better. Imagine how pleasing it is for God to hear us worship Him with such abandon. So, lift up your voice and sing loudly. (Just ask God, that those who hear your voice would hear music in their ears.) After all, it's more important to please God.

~Tanya J.

3 things I am thankful for today:

1.____________________

2.____________________

3.____________________

What is one thing God wants me to do for Him today?

Listening with Calm Stillness

God's not asking for physical stillness, but for me to allow my mind to stop and take a rest, to stop taking action in my thoughts and with my mouth, to let God be the one in our relationship who is active. How? Complete trust, faith, and accepting the truth. Apart from God, I can do nothing good.

~Debi S.

"Be still, and know that I am God;"

Psalm 46:10

3 things I am thankful for today:

1.____________________

2.____________________

3.____________________

What is one thing God wants me to do for Him today?

Deliverance

"Now is my soul troubled; and what shall I say? Father, save me from this hour: but for this cause came I unto this hour."

John 12.27 (KJV)

Jesus did not ask to be delivered from the cross because that was His purpose for coming. The Bible tell us that Jesus endured the cross, rejecting the shame because of the joy set before Him. Had Jesus not suffered death on the cross we could not be saved. Maybe in difficult times we should look for how those times will benefit others rather than asking God to deliver us from the difficulty.

~Steve R.

3 things I am thankful for today:

1.____________________

2.____________________

3.____________________

What is one thing God wants me to do for Him today?

Pleasing in Your Sight

So many times, I just blow it. I say things and do things that are just wrong. This verse has been my prayer so many times as I repent and seek God's face and forgiveness. Realizing repentance is not just regret, but a change in heart direction and that comes through meditating on God's Word and then following it.

~Betty W.

"May these words of my mouth and this meditation of my heart be pleasing in your sight, Lord, my Rock and my Redeemer."

Psalm 19:14

3 things I am thankful for today:

1.____________________

2.____________________

3.____________________

What is one thing God wants me to do for Him today?

Choose God Over Bitterness

"May our Lord Jesus Christ himself and God our Father, who loved us and by his grace gave us eternal encouragement and good hope, encourage your hearts and strengthen you in every good deed and word."

2 Thessalonians 2:16-17

Christ is the answer to sorrow. When I learned that my grandsons had perished in the Oklahoma City Bombing, there were two courses open to me: give way to despair and become bitter and angry, or turn to God. Trusting God changed my life and saved me from a life of misery.

~Kathy S.

3 things I am thankful for today:

1.____________________

2.____________________

3.____________________

What is one thing God wants me to do for Him today?

Too Weak to Form Words

When we plummet into a black hole of fearful uncertainty, going to God shows we're depending on Him, trusting in His way, in His timing, and in whatever way He has chosen to work in our intense painful situation. The Holy Spirit takes our moans and tears to our Heavenly Father who is bringing "all things" together for His glory.

~Ruth N.

"the Spirit helps us in our weakness. We do not know what we ought to pray for, but the Spirit himself intercedes for us through wordless groans. And he who searches our hearts knows the mind of the Spirit, because the Spirit intercedes for God's people in accordance with the will of God."

Romans 8:26-27

3 things I am thankful for today:

1.____________________

2.____________________

3.____________________

What is one thing God wants me to do for Him today?

Claim Your Prize

"...Always give yourselves fully to the work of the Lord, because you know that your labor in the Lord is not in vain."

1 Corinthians 15:58

When we do good works or charitable acts for others, (which, I expect comes naturally for most of us) we don't think about receiving anything in return. However, we as Christians are doing it for the Lord, and He has a place for us behind those pearly gates as a reward for our faithfulness.

~LunaGram

3 things I am thankful for today:

1.____________________

2.____________________

3.____________________

What is one thing God wants me to do for Him today?

Be a Seeker

Fear is an unpleasant feeling triggered by the perception of danger, real or imagined. We've all been in fear's grip – paralyzed, consumed, and controlled by people or situations. By seeking God, the chains are broken, progress is made, and peace is restored. Fear filled today? Seek the Lord!

~Reba L.

"I sought the Lord, and he answered me; he delivered me from all my fears."

Psalm 34:4

3 things I am thankful for today:

1.____________________

2.____________________

3.____________________

What is one thing God wants me to do for Him today?

Freed Up to Love

"You, my brothers and sisters, were called to be free. But do not use your freedom to indulge the flesh; rather, serve one another humbly in love. For the entire law is fulfilled in keeping this one command: 'Love your neighbor as yourself.'"

Galatians 5:13-15

We believe God created us in love and in Jesus has freed us from the lethal impact of sin and our inadequate abilities to live in harmony with God and His creatures. God's only expectation is that we use our freedom to benefit others, as we have benefited from His love.

~Jim H.

3 things I am thankful for today:

1.____________________

2.____________________

3.____________________

What is one thing God wants me to do for Him today?

The Big Fight

Have you ever wrestled with God? I mean really struggled with Him over an event or situation in your life. He is always ready for the fight because He really cares. He seems to say, "I know exactly how you feel. Let it out! I can take it!" Then, when the fight is over, He tenderly mends our wounds and carries us onward.

~Becky M.

"So Jacob was left alone, and a man wrestled with him till daybreak…So Jacob called the place Peniel, saying, 'It is because I saw God face to face, and yet my life was spared.'"

Genesis 32:24,30

3 things I am thankful for today:

1.____________________

2.____________________

3.____________________

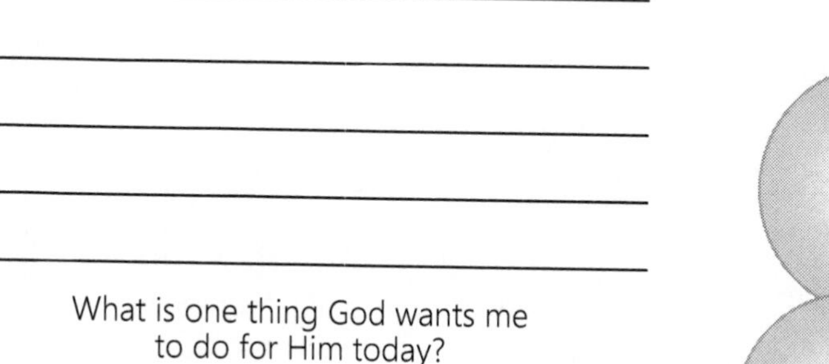

What is one thing God wants me to do for Him today?

You Are Always Loved

"For I am convinced that neither death nor life, neither angels nor demons, neither the present nor the future, nor any powers, neither height nor depth, nor anything else in all creation, will be able to separate us from the love of God that is in Christ Jesus our Lord."

Romans 8:38-39

Most of people's worries come from feeling unloved. Be comforted in the wisdom that God will always love you. God will never abandon or forsake you. We often make things worse than they can possibly be, but God will let us know the way and the truth. We should never fear the unknown for Jesus is with us.

~Donna P.

3 things I am thankful for today:

1.______________________________

2.______________________________

3.______________________________

What is one thing God wants me to do for Him today?

What is Required of Me?

God is so gracious to guide and lead us. He knows what is good and gives us the blueprint on how to live: act justly; love mercy; and walk humbly with Him.

~Julie K.

"He has shown you, O mortal, what is good. And what does the Lord require of you? To act justly and to love mercy and to walk humbly with your God."

Micah 6:8

3 things I am thankful for today:

1.________________

2.________________

3.________________

What is one thing God wants me to do for Him today?

Victory of Deliverance

"If we are thrown into the blazing furnace, the God we serve is able to deliver us from it, and he will deliver us from Your Majesty's hand."

Daniel 3:17

For Shadrach, Meshach, and Abednego, God didn't put out the fire – He just put Jesus in there with them! It's not about God putting out your fires; it's about who is in there with you. The furnace represents the victory of people standing up for what they believe and refusing to bow to oppression.

~Peggy H.

3 things I am thankful for today:

1.________________________

2.________________________

3.________________________

What is one thing God wants me to do for Him today?

My Heart Leaps for Joy

I have never gone through trials alone. Sometimes, I need God to help me walk through them. I need His strength. Sometimes, I need Him to shield me from having to struggle through some trial. He knows what I can endure and He is with me. My heart trusts in Him, and I have never had Him fail me.

~Marilyn C.

"The Lord is my strength and my shield; my heart trusts in him, and he helps me. My heart leaps for joy, and with my song I praise him"

Psalm 28:7

3 things I am thankful for today:

1.________________

2.________________

3.________________

What is one thing God wants me to do for Him today?

Compassion

"Carry each other's burdens, and in this way you will fulfill the law of Christ."

Galatians 6:2

The Village is a caring place. Great love of the Lord and deep faith abide here in the "buckle" of the Bible Belt. I've seen faith and love in action as residents give their help, care, and kindness to various charitable causes...including (unexpectedly) to me, as I grieved for my loved one.

~Susan M.

3 things I am thankful for today:

1.________________

2.________________

3.________________

What is one thing God wants me to do for Him today?

Toothpaste Out of the Tube

How many times have you wanted to take back something that you said? A hurtful statement or a partial truth can prey on one's conscience. We want to shine for God, but our tongue can actually cause our brother to stumble. Let's take a deep breath and think about what we say before we say it.

~Vickie H.

"Those who consider themselves religious and yet do not keep a tight rein on their tongues deceive themselves, and their religion is worthless."

James 1:26

3 things I am thankful for today:

1.____________________

2.____________________

3.____________________

What is one thing God wants me to do for Him today?

Strength Through Adversity

"...we also glory in our sufferings, because we know that suffering produces perseverance;"

Romans 5:3

Take heart when you are confronted with adversity. God is molding you for His purpose. Do not despair. Be confident that through suffering God will make you stronger. Consider when you begin an exercise routine, your muscles ache for a while, but in time your strength increases. So it is with adversity.

~Debbie R.

3 things I am thankful for today:

1.____________________

2.____________________

3.____________________

What is one thing God wants me to do for Him today?

Definitions

Micah 6:8 is simple, yet challenging. Defining the "right," the "good," and being "humble" before God seems to be subjective and relative in our culture today. Is it possible for us all or even most of us to agree on the definitions? I fear not, but believing in hope, patience, tolerance, and a generous spirit will take us far.

~Paula D.

"He has shown you, O mortal, what is good. And what does the Lord require of you? To act justly and to love mercy and to walk humbly with your God."

Micah 6:8

3 things I am thankful for today:

1.__________

2.__________

3.__________

What is one thing God wants me to do for Him today?

Eyes Everywhere

"You know when I sit
and when I rise;
you perceive my
thoughts from afar."

Psalm 139:2

As a youngster, if I got caught doing something I shouldn't, I would ask Momma how she knew. She said she had eyes everywhere. Well, this is a gazillion times bigger than that...God knows everything about me, even my thoughts!

~Teela Y.

3 things I am thankful for today:

1.__________

2.__________

3.__________

What is one thing God wants me to do for Him today?

Strengthening Faith

Lifting weights is hard work, but over time, the constant lifting produces strong muscles. Likewise, giving glory to God, even while living in a seemingly impossible situation, is hard to do. But, the more we give "glory to God," the stronger our faith muscles grow. Stronger faith muscles produce steadfastness to live for God until He calls us home.

~Ruth N.

"Yet he did not waver through unbelief regarding the promise of God, but was strengthened in his faith and gave glory to God,"
Romans 4:20

____
____
____
____
____
____
____
____
____
____
____
____
____
____
____
____

3 things I am thankful for today:

1.____________________
2.____________________
3.____________________

What is one thing God wants me to do for Him today?

____

Praise Him

"I will sing the Lord's praise, for he has been good to me."
Psalm 13:6

Looking in the rear-view mirror of our life, we see how God has provided; He has made us grow. But we can't drive looking backward. We need to keep our eyes forward on Jesus. Tell others of His goodness. Sing songs of praise to our God. Tell of His wonderful provision.

~Chris C.

3 things I am thankful for today:

1.________________

2.________________

3.________________

What is one thing God wants me to do for Him today?

10. Angels Among Us

by Steve Wilhite

During the summer of 1994, our family embarked on the perfect family vacation. Our children, ages seven and five, were very excited. We all loved the lake. We loved boating and spent weeks planning our first camping trip at Lake Powell.

It was a perfect picture – mom driving the SUV towing the boat, 5-year-old Corby in the front passenger seat (it was legal back then!), and dad and son in back making plans for the weekend: fishing, hiking, boating, tubing, swimming, laughing, singing, and eating hot dogs. We were ready for fun!

First came a weird noise, followed by the wildest roller coaster ride you could imagine! The car swerved, ricocheted, rocked, rolled, hit a guardrail, then rolled multiple times and flipped! We were too overwhelmed to scream, wondering what the heck had happened. The SUV finally became still, passenger-side-down, on Interstate 40. In total bewilderment, we realized we were okay. Maybe that was the biggest shock of all! Our injuries were minor: Corby had bitten her tongue and I had a scratch on my leg.

After the highway patrol arrived, pieces of the bizarre incident began unfolding like a Hollywood movie. We had been hit by a drunk driver, who had been fleeing in a truck on three wheels. She tested .22 alcohol level (the legal limit is .08) and, eventually, passed out in the police car. We could hardly believe we had survived such a frightful accident.

I had been walking up and down the highway gathering up our belongings when my wife, Betty, told me that Corby had seen an angel.

We all believed strongly in God. Jesus was the Lord of our lives, and Betty and I were always thrilled at our children's faith (and still are…). But an angel? Corby was young, so we would never let her think we doubted her. I got down on her level, looked her straight in the eyes and said, "What color was the angel?" White was her answer. I smiled; the truck that hit us was white. She smiled as only a 5-year-old can and very matter-of-factly said, "It was not a truck I saw. It was an ANGEL!"

Months later, Corby told her story to a friend who was a pastor, recounting it exactly as she had the day of the accident. Again and again, she described her angel:. white, male in appearance, and standing at the guardrail with his hands up. The pastor even said, "Corby, don't you mean 'she' was standing at the guardrail?

Angels are usually depicted as being female." There was no shaking Corby; her angel was male, just like Gabriel and Michael.

Corby is now 35 years old and this story has not lost one ounce of its credibility. We believe in angels and thank God that He sent one to look over us that summer. Otherwise, maybe none of us would be here today to tell this story and of His great love.

> *"For he will command his angels concerning you to guard you in all your ways;"* Psalm 91:11

> *"'He will command his angels concerning you, and they will lift you up in their hands, so that you will not strike your foot against a stone.'"* Matthew 4:6

Kindness Counts

Whenever my faith is faltering or my hope is dimming, I am reminded that my faith and my hope are in God and His great love for me. Sharing His love is the greatest act I can do as a Christian! Even the smallest acts of kindness count in God's eyes!

~Debbie C.

"And now these three remain: faith, hope and love. But the greatest of these is love."

1 Corinthians 13:13

3 things I am thankful for today:

1.____________________

2.____________________

3.____________________

What is one thing God wants me to do for Him today?

Please Let My Light Shine

"In the same way, let your light shine before others, that they may see your good deeds and glorify your Father in heaven."

Matthew 5:16

I look all around me and see my friends. Their shining lights bring me closer to You. Their wisdom has taught me, their kindness has encouraged me, their godly examples have shown me what "Christ in you" really looks like. Please, God, let my light shine, so that others will glorify You.

~JoNancy S.

3 things I am thankful for today:

1.____________________

2.____________________

3.____________________

What is one thing God wants me to do for Him today?

Pay Special Attention

So many needs – what can I really do? St. Augustine says, "You are to pay special attention to those who, by the accidents of time, or place, or circumstances, are brought into closer connection with you." Look at those God brings you in touch with; pick one need, and meet it. God brings folks across our paths for a reason. You honor Him by meeting one need at a time.

~Marilyn C.

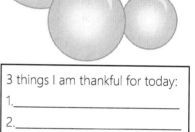

"Dear children, let us not love with words or speech but with actions and in truth."

1 John 3:18

3 things I am thankful for today:

1.____________________

2.____________________

3.____________________

What is one thing God wants me to do for Him today?

Signs

"Jesus performed many other signs in the presence of his disciples, which are not recorded in this book. But these are written that you may believe that Jesus is the Messiah, the Son of God, and that by believing you may have life in his name."

John 20:30-31

I wonder about all those other signs that Jesus did while He was on earth. Were they big miracles? Were they small? Who was the recipient? I need to remember to look around and see the signs that God is doing in my life daily!

~Julie K.

3 things I am thankful for today:

1.____________________

2.____________________

3.____________________

What is one thing God wants me to do for Him today?

The Human Family

In the grand scheme of things, the color of our skin and the shape of our eyes count for so little. We all laugh and cry, thirst and hunger, celebrate and mourn. With this knowledge comes the understanding that we are all a part of something greater—the human family.

~Kathy S.

"'A new command I give you: Love one another. As I have loved you, so you must love one another.'"

John 13:34

3 things I am thankful for today:

1.________________

2.________________

3.________________

What is one thing God wants me to do for Him today?

God's Got This

"Cast all your anxiety on him because he cares for you."
1 Peter 5:7

The loss of a spouse to illness, then death, can shake you to your very core. Having been half of a couple for years, then finding yourself on your own, can play havoc with your sense of identity. Who am I now? What path has God planned for me? What a comfort to know that God's controlling the journey.

~Susan M.

3 things I am thankful for today:

1.____________________

2.____________________

3.____________________

What is one thing God wants me to do for Him today?

Pass It On!

One hot summer day at the library, I had a dead battery. A stranger offered to help, then drove me to purchase a new one. When I got ready to pay, he took out his checkbook and paid for my battery. After helping me install the new one, he simply said, "Pass it on" and drove away. To this day, I look for ways to "Pass it on!"

~Steve B.

"The King will reply, 'Truly I tell you, whatever you did for one of the least of these brothers and sisters of mine, you did for me.'"

Matthew 25:40

3 things I am thankful for today:

1.____________________

2.____________________

3.____________________

What is one thing God wants me to do for Him today?

Stormy Weather

"He replied, 'You of little faith, why are you so afraid?' Then he got up and rebuked the winds and the waves, and it was completely calm."

Matthew 8:26

None of us escapes this life without storms. When we reach retirement age, like many Villagers have, the storms can be about health, finances, family, or a multitude of other reasons. Even if you feel alone, remember that God is with you throughout all the storms of your life.

~Rita T.

3 things I am thankful for today:

1.____________________

2.____________________

3.____________________

What is one thing God wants me to do for Him today?

Worries About Our Children

How many of us worry over the welfare of our children? Whether it is concern for their souls or their physical well-being, it is anxiety! I lived this fear for many years before I came to the realization the our Lord could protect them far better than I. Releasing them into the loving arms of our Lord brought peace!

~Rose F.

"Which of you, if your son asks for bread, will give him a stone? Or if he asks for a fish, will give him a snake? If you, then, though you are evil, know how to give good gifts to your children, how much more will your Father in heaven give good gifts to those who ask him!

Matthew 7:9-11

3 things I am thankful for today:

1.____________________

2.____________________

3.____________________

What is one thing God wants me to do for Him today?

Fear Not!

"So do not fear, for I am with you; do not be dismayed, for I am your God. I will strengthen you and help you; I will uphold you with my righteous right hand."

Isaiah 41:10

We all have fears, some large and some small. Even small fears, like my fear of spiders, can be very hard to overcome! God understands, because He offers us reassurance over 80 times in His Word that we do not need to fear! God is willing and able to help us and protect us in any circumstances. Fear not!

~Debbie C.

3 things I am thankful for today:

1.__________

2.__________

3.__________

What is one thing God wants me to do for Him today?

Be Transformed

In Conway, Arkansas, there is a group of wonderful ladies who take broken china pieces and make them into beautiful necklace pendants, with all proceeds benefitting the Women's Shelter of Central Arkansas. Their motto is "Broken dishes renewed, broken lives transformed."

~Peggy H.

"Do not conform to the pattern of this world, but be transformed by the renewing of your mind. Then you will be able to test and approve what God's will is– his good, pleasing and perfect will."
Romans 12:2

3 things I am thankful for today:

1.____________________

2.____________________

3.____________________

What is one thing God wants me to do for Him today?

Total Confidence

"in God I trust and
am not afraid.
What can man do to me?"
Psalm 56:11

King David always had total confidence in God. As a mere boy, he killed a fierce giant with a pebble! That should have been enough to inspire everlasting confidence. Well, we have the same God – still here, still inspiring confidence. Look around and you will be astonished at His glory all about you. And then look up!

~Warren W.

3 things I am thankful for today:

1.________________

2.________________

3.________________

What is one thing God wants me to do for Him today?

Surrender + Trust = Peace

No matter where you are in the world, God's presence is always with you. Our Father's unconditional love is just waiting for you to receive it. He thinks you are worth it! The ultimate gift is peace that is achieved by total surrender and trust.

~Marty S.

"But I trust in you, Lord; I say, "You are my God." My times are in your hands; deliver me from the hands of my enemies, from those who pursue me. Let your face shine on your servant; save me in your unfailing love."

Psalm 31:14-16

3 things I am thankful for today:

1.____________________

2.____________________

3.____________________

What is one thing God wants me to do for Him today?

Quiet Words of a Wise Man

"The words of a wise man are heard in quiet more than the cry of him that ruleth among fools."
Ecclesiastes 9:17 (KJV)

A wise man has learned it is better to speak quietly rather than ranting like a fool. No one wants to hear yelling and screaming. If something important is to be said, being well-prepared and speaking in a calm voice is much better. Words spoken in anger are usually regretted.

~Suzan R.

3 things I am thankful for today:

1.____________________

2.____________________

3.____________________

What is one thing God wants me to do for Him today?

Doing My Piece for Peace

There is a song that says, let there be peace on earth and let it begin with me. Sometimes, we can feel that what we do won't make much difference, but God disagrees! He doesn't expect us to solve all the world's problems, but He does expect us to do our part to promote peace, even if it is just within our own family.

~Debbie C.

"If it is possible, as far as it depends on you, live at peace with everyone."

Romans 12:18

3 things I am thankful for today:

1.____________________

2.____________________

3.____________________

What is one thing God wants me to do for Him today?

Let Us Rejoice!

"The Lord has done it this very day; let us rejoice today and be glad."

Psalm 118:24

An earlier version (King James) of this verse says, "This is the day that the Lord has made. Let us rejoice and be glad in it." What a magnificent way to start everyday. Because He has proven Himself faithful in the past, we can trust the Lord for the unknown future. One day at a time!

~JoNancy S.

3 things I am thankful for today:

1.____________________

2.____________________

3.____________________

What is one thing God wants me to do for Him today?

We Don't Create Love, We Share It

What a relief! I don't have to concoct or invent love. It's already here, demonstrated by God's love to create us, give us free will, rescue us, and send a constant spiritual supporter. All I need to do is share God's love with every person I encounter.

~Jim H.

"We love because he first loved us. Whoever claims to love God yet hates a brother or sister is a liar. For whoever does not love their brother and sister, whom they have seen, cannot love God, whom they have not seen. And he has given us this command: Anyone who loves God must also love their brother and sister."

1 John 4:19-21

3 things I am thankful for today:

1.__________

2.__________

3.__________

What is one thing God wants me to do for Him today?

Jesus Loves Me, Rewritten

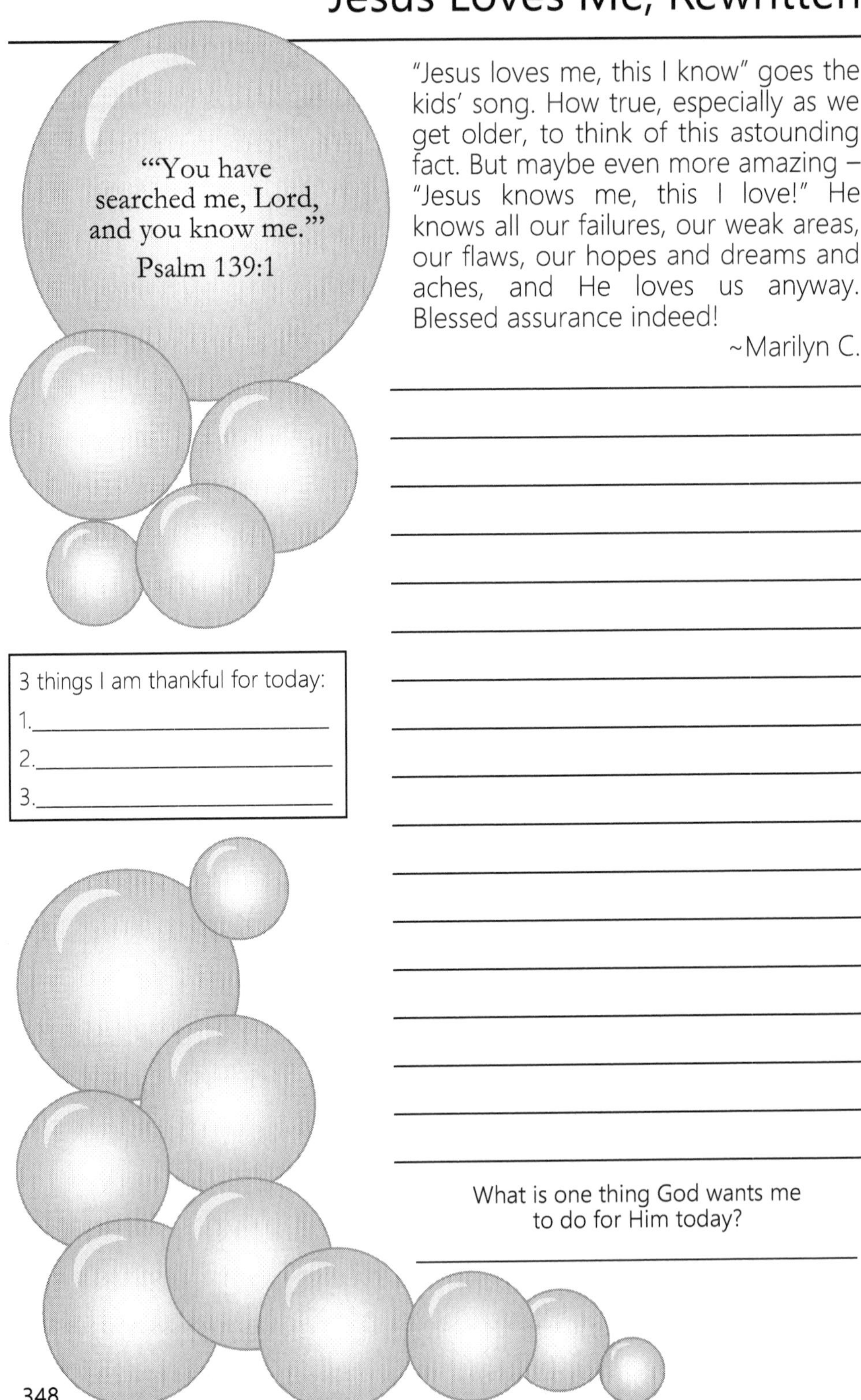

"'You have searched me, Lord, and you know me.'"
Psalm 139:1

"Jesus loves me, this I know" goes the kids' song. How true, especially as we get older, to think of this astounding fact. But maybe even more amazing – "Jesus knows me, this I love!" He knows all our failures, our weak areas, our flaws, our hopes and dreams and aches, and He loves us anyway. Blessed assurance indeed!

~Marilyn C.

3 things I am thankful for today:

1.____________________

2.____________________

3.____________________

What is one thing God wants me to do for Him today?

There is Hope for Prodigals

When I consider the prodigals in my life, I can take comfort knowing they were taught well in their early years. What happened after? Can I blame our society today, our education system, the individual's weakness of character, or is it simply one's self-will? The Bible tells us that these children do come back and follow Jesus. Let us hope.

~Debbie R.

"Start children off on the way they should go, and even when they are old they will not turn from it."

Proverbs 22:6

3 things I am thankful for today:

1.____________________

2.____________________

3.____________________

What is one thing God wants me to do for Him today?

Be Strong and Courageous

"Have I not commanded you? Be strong and courageous. Do not be afraid; do not be discouraged, for the Lord your God will be with you wherever you go."

Joshua 1:9

While whitewater rafting down the Royal Gorge, we hit Class 5 rapids. I was thankful for my helmet, but more thankful that my husband was in front of me. Having him there gave me courage. Having God with us should make us strong and courageous.

~Teela Y.

3 things I am thankful for today:

1.____________________

2.____________________

3.____________________

What is one thing God wants me to do for Him today?

God is My Rock

Having suffered with fibromyalgia and degeneration of the spine since childhood, I have had people ask how I continue to do so much. I tell them, "God is my strength, my ROCK!" The Holy Spirit lifts me up. Also, prayer covering is so important; I have prayer warriors in my life and I feel their support. Be someone's prayer warrior today.

~Phillis R.

"In all your ways submit to him, and he will make your paths straight."

Proverbs 3:6

3 things I am thankful for today:

1.____________________

2.____________________

3.____________________

What is one thing God wants me to do for Him today?

We Are All One in Christ

"There is neither Jew nor Gentile, neither slave nor free, nor is there male and female, for you are all one in Christ Jesus."

Galatians 3:28

While Jesus was on this earth, He set the example of how we should view others. He reached out to people from all walks of life. He even touched the "untouchables" (lepers) and ate dinner with despised tax collectors! No matter where a person is from, their social standing, gender, age, etc., we are loved as we are and invited to believe and be a part of God's Kingdom, where all are one in Christ.

~Debbie C.

3 things I am thankful for today:

1.____________________

2.____________________

3.____________________

What is one thing God wants me to do for Him today?

A Glimpse of Heaven

Perhaps it is in the sweet presence of children, with their innocent laughter and enduring smiles, that we gain a glimpse of heaven.

~Kathy S.

"When I consider your heavens, the work of your fingers, the moon and the stars, which you have set in place,"

Psalm 8:3

3 things I am thankful for today:

1.____________________

2.____________________

3.____________________

What is one thing God wants me to do for Him today?

Stand Your Ground

"Therefore put on the full armor of God, so that when the day of evil comes, you may be able to stand your ground, and after you have done everything, to stand."

Ephesians 6:13

When your world is falling apart, when friends desert you, when temptation becomes too tempting, and you must stand or fall, the armor of God will give you the strength to stand. And when all is done, to still stand. Anyone can choose to sit down and give up. That's easy. Standing requires faith and effort.

~Diane G.

3 things I am thankful for today:

1.____________________

2.____________________

3.____________________

What is one thing God wants me to do for Him today?

Even in Troubled Waters

God does not promise that He will protect us from all troubles. His word says, "When you pass through the waters." But He does promise we won't go through them alone. He will be there. You may be in a place in your life where you feel close to being overwhelmed. Cling to Him like you would grab a branch in the midst of a raging river. He will hold you when the waters churn.

~Marilyn C.

"When you pass through the waters, I will be with you; and when you pass through the rivers, they will not sweep over you."

Isaiah 43:2

3 things I am thankful for today:

1.__________

2.__________

3.__________

What is one thing God wants me to do for Him today?

The Wind of Faith

"Now faith is confidence in what we hope for and assurance about what we do not see."
Hebrews 11:1

Some say, "How can I believe in what I cannot see or touch," but that's exactly what Faith is – trusting in your heart what you cannot see or touch. You can't see wind, but you can see its effect on things around you. Faith is like wind, with God wrapping you in His embrace, exhilarating you, and leaving you wanting to learn more.

~Tanya J.

3 things I am thankful for today:

1.__________

2.__________

3.__________

What is one thing God wants me to do for Him today?

Village Friends

Friendships in The Village are something special. Is it that most of us are now retired, with more time to devote to one another than we had, back when life was full of child-raising and career-building? Whatever the reason, it's a blessing, the way we rejoice in each others' good fortune and help each other in tough times.

~Susan M.

"Therefore encourage one another and build each other up, just as in fact you are doing."

1 Thessalonians 5:11

3 things I am thankful for today:

1.________________

2.________________

3.________________

What is one thing God wants me to do for Him today?

Religion and Politics

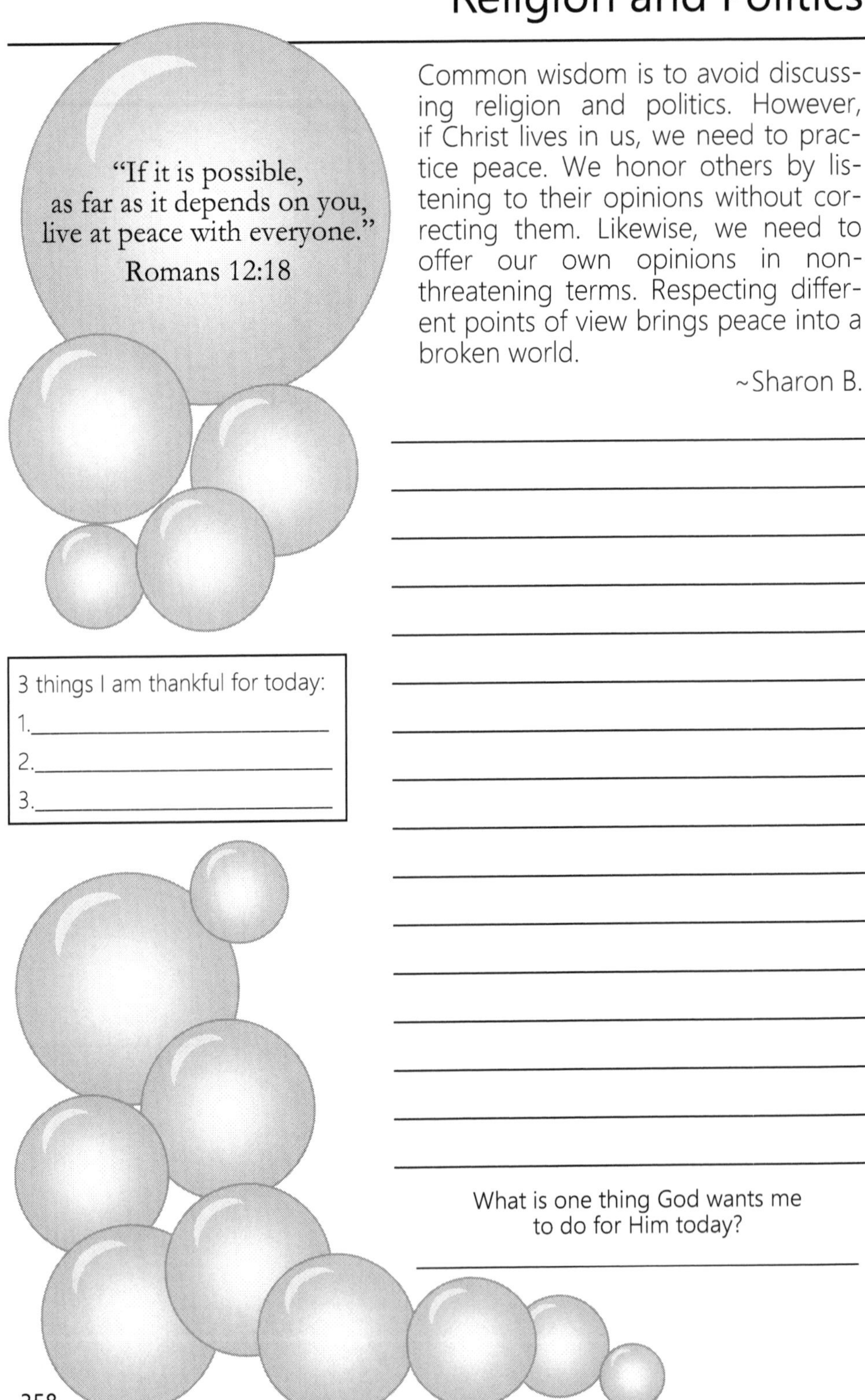

"If it is possible,
as far as it depends on you,
live at peace with everyone."
Romans 12:18

Common wisdom is to avoid discussing religion and politics. However, if Christ lives in us, we need to practice peace. We honor others by listening to their opinions without correcting them. Likewise, we need to offer our own opinions in non-threatening terms. Respecting different points of view brings peace into a broken world.

~Sharon B.

3 things I am thankful for today:

1.____________________________

2.____________________________

3.____________________________

What is one thing God wants me to do for Him today?

No More Tears

One thing different about living in Hot Springs Village is that the median age is a lot older than in other communities. We say goodbye too soon to many of our friends. It will be awesome in Heaven when there will be no more death, mourning, crying, and pain. And especially, no more tears!

~Julie K

"He will wipe every tear from their eyes. There will be no more death or mourning or crying or pain, for the old order of things has passed away."

Revelation 21:4

3 things I am thankful for today:

1.____________________

2.____________________

3.____________________

What is one thing God wants me to do for Him today?

Don’t Give In to the Dirt!

“Finally, brothers and sisters, whatever is true, whatever is noble, whatever is right, whatever is pure, whatever is lovely, whatever is admirable–if anything is excellent or praiseworthy–think about such things.”

Philippians 4:8

Sometimes this world we live in can seem like a "dirty" place! It can be very disappointing, discouraging, and downright depressing! God, however, tells us that we are not to focus on the "dirt," but, as followers who have our hope in Him, we are to look for the good, the things and people worthy of praise. So look around, focus on the good, and don't give in to the "dirt"!

~Debbie C.

3 things I am thankful for today:

1.____________________

2.____________________

3.____________________

What is one thing God wants me to do for Him today?

Never Alone

He is my strength! Nothing defines "alone" like becoming a widow. First, childless...now husband-less, as well. Weariness is overwhelming; the aloneness unending. But He promises to strengthen and protect. Proven repeatedly now for 26 years. I am NOT alone – EVER! Praise God!

~JoNancy S.

"But the Lord is faithful, and he will strengthen you and protect you from the evil one."

2 Thessalonians 3:3

3 things I am thankful for today:

1.____________________

2.____________________

3.____________________

What is one thing God wants me to do for Him today?

11. The SCAT Family

by Lynda Grasse

What would you do if someone took your car keys away and told you that you'll never be able to drive again? Compound that by residing in the middle of 26,000 wooded acres with only winding, hilly roads, no sidewalks, and no public transportation.

God's hand was at work when Patty MacDonald and Lynda Grasse met one evening in 2006 at a social gathering. Patty had lived in Hot Springs Village for years; she knew hundreds of people. Lynda was new to the Village, but she had established a nonprofit transportation service at her church in Wisconsin. HSV SCAT was conceived that very evening!

SCAT? To this day, people say, "What an awful name!" Let's just say it's an awful name for a much needed, wonderful service. South Central Arkansas Transit, operated by the Central Arkansas Development Council, provides rides for people in the Village. The all volunteer staff of schedulers and drivers are unique in the state of Arkansas.

Village SCAT's goal is to help individuals remain independent. Currently, 63 volunteers provide 275 rides per month, operating 2-3 vans 75% of the time. When a rider says, "Thank you! I could not live in my home without Village SCAT to take me to the doctor and shopping," is the proof of SCAT's success.

When Ray, a favorite and faithful rider, passed away recently, his wife called the next morning with a most unique request, "Would SCAT provide one more ride for my husband?" When the SCAT van arrived at the funeral home, Ray's ashes were placed where he always insisted on riding – the front seat! Destination: the church and beyond!

Alongside the scenery, nature, recreation, clubs, and serenity offered by HSV are residents who care and are eager to volunteer. Drivers and schedulers are dedicated to helping neighbors. Many stories can be told that show God's love:

- Helping a low-vision rider pick out greeting cards
- Transporting a resident in the wheelchair van to Thanksgiving dinner -even though SCAT is closed on Thanksgiving.
- Paying for groceries when a rider left their money at home
- Listening to riders' challenges and life stories

- Going far beyond their volunteer duties, i.e. painting a deck or visiting in hospitals

SCAT is a perfect example of how God provides for His own. He does not look for volunteers well equipped to do His work. He seeks willing servants who will join Him. He does the equipping.

"The King will reply, 'Truly I tell you, whatever you did for one of the least of these brothers and sisters of mine, you did for me.'" Matthew 25:40

"Each of you should use whatever gift you have received to serve others, as faithful stewards of God's grace in its various forms." 1 Peter 4:10

Don't Do It for the Thanks

There are so many opportunities to help, so many claims on our time and resources. Discernment is necessary or end up just helping the noisiest seekers. As Christians, we want to rescue everyone, putting ourselves in God's place. We need to prayerfully approach our service opportunities, matching our gifts and our limitations to the needs. And we shouldn't do it for the thanks!

~Sharon B.

"Let us not become weary in doing good, for at the proper time we will reap a harvest if we do not give up."

Galatians 6:9

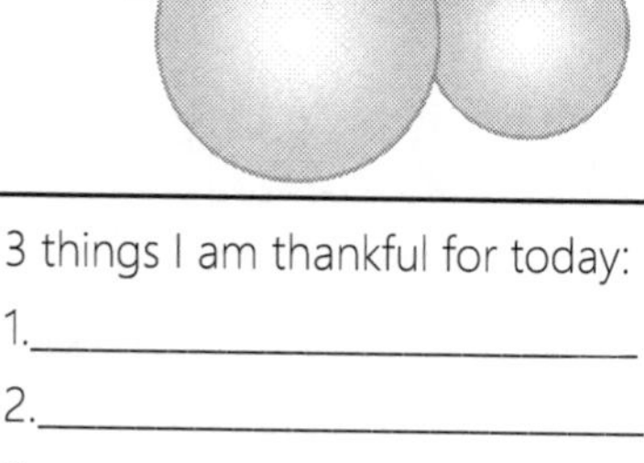

3 things I am thankful for today:

1.____________________

2.____________________

3.____________________

What is one thing God wants me to do for Him today?

Walk in Faith

"For we live by faith,
not by sight."
2 Corinthians 5:7

A faith-walk is taken one step at a time, leaning on God as much as we need. This is not a path of frequent success but many failures. However, each failure is followed by growth and nourished by He who leads me to a blessed victorious life.

~Donna P.

3 things I am thankful for today:

1.________________________

2.________________________

3.________________________

What is one thing God wants me to do for Him today?

It Takes a Village

With age, I have come to accept the fact I can't always do things by myself, and often have to ask for help. God has equipped each of us with different gifts so that together, as one complete Christian family body, we can accomplish the tasks He has set before us.

~Jody M.

"so in Christ we, though many, form one body, and each member belongs to all the others."

Romans 12:5

3 things I am thankful for today:

1.__________

2.__________

3.__________

What is one thing God wants me to do for Him today?

The Fig Tree

"And Peter calling to remembrance saith unto him, Master, behold, the fig tree which thou cursedst is withered away."

Mark 11:21 (KJV)

Lessons:

1. Jesus made all things including this tree.
2. Jesus knew it wasn't time for figs.
3. Trees don't have a free will. It would have been doing exactly what God had planned for it to do.
4. Just as God used the fig tree for His purpose, He has the right to use us in any way He sees fit. .

~Steve R.

3 things I am thankful for today:

1.________________________

2.________________________

3.________________________

What is one thing God wants me to do for Him today?

The Very Best Family

Our backgrounds and family lives, are not perfect. Some of us come from places of deep hurt or dysfunction, but for those of us who know Jesus Christ, that has all changed! We have been lovingly welcomed into the greatest family possible. God does not just save us grudgingly, out of pity for our sorry state. He lavishes love on us. He claims us; He adopts us as His kids!

~Marilyn C.

"See what great love the Father has lavished on us, that we should be called children of God! And that is what we are! …"

1 John 3:1

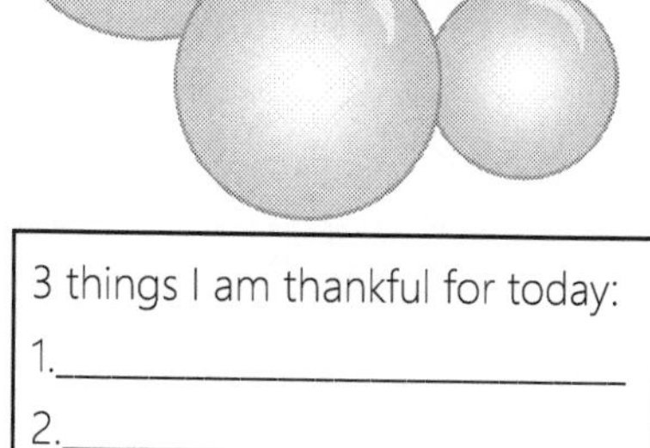

3 things I am thankful for today:

1.____________________

2.____________________

3.____________________

What is one thing God wants me to do for Him today?

Talking Out of Turn

"Do not let any unwholesome talk come out of your mouths, but only what is helpful for building others up according to their needs, that it may benefit those who listen."

Ephesians 4:29

All of us have said things that we wish we could push right back in our mouths. Once, when we got lost in Las Vegas, I lashed out at my family due to my own frustrations. I was sorry immediately and asked forgiveness. I thank God for my Christian (forgiving) family members and my merciful God.

~Phillis R.

3 things I am thankful for today:

1.____________________

2.____________________

3.____________________

What is one thing God wants me to do for Him today?

God is Worthy!

Sometimes, we can lose sight of our purpose here on earth. We become discouraged and wonder why we're even here. We are here because it is God's will! I am here because of God's will!! Rejoice and bring glory to God. Only then will we find true meaning in our lives.

~Betty W.

"You are worthy, our Lord and God, to receive glory and honor and power, for you created all things, and by your will they were created and have their being."

Revelation 4:11

3 things I am thankful for today:

1.________________

2.________________

3.________________

What is one thing God wants me to do for Him today?

A Mother's Prayer

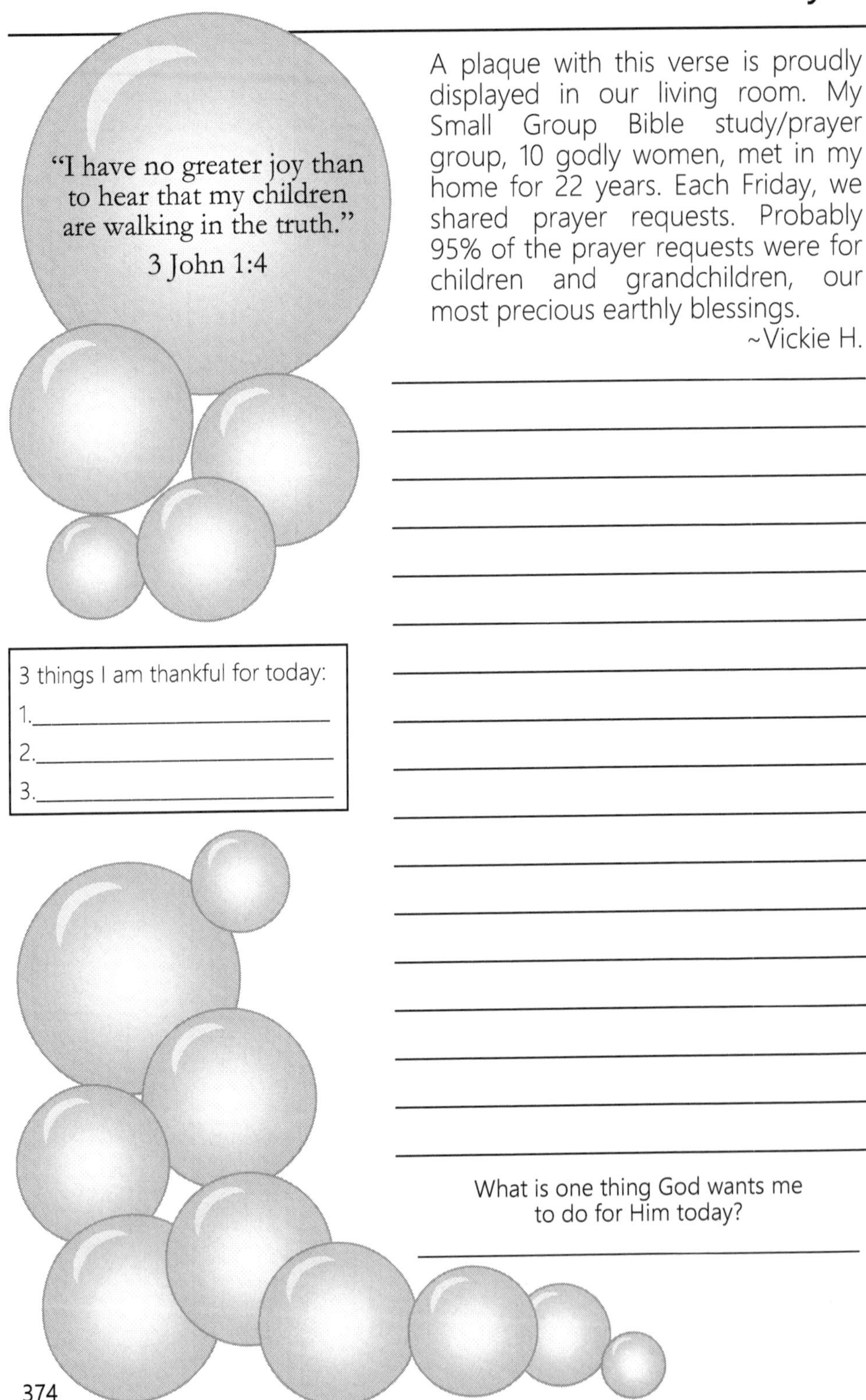

"I have no greater joy than to hear that my children are walking in the truth."
3 John 1:4

A plaque with this verse is proudly displayed in our living room. My Small Group Bible study/prayer group, 10 godly women, met in my home for 22 years. Each Friday, we shared prayer requests. Probably 95% of the prayer requests were for children and grandchildren, our most precious earthly blessings.

~Vickie H.

3 things I am thankful for today:

1.____________________

2.____________________

3.____________________

What is one thing God wants me to do for Him today?

No Retirees

I love the fact that God has prepared good works for us to do. He knows what skills and talents He has given us and He has jobs and tasks for us to accomplish. So, even though we may be retired from the workforce, God still has work for us to do! We are never retired from God's workforce.

~Julie K

"For we are God's handiwork, created in Christ Jesus to do good works, which God prepared in advance for us to do."

Ephesians 2:10

3 things I am thankful for today:

1.____________________

2.____________________

3.____________________

What is one thing God wants me to do for Him today?

Help is Here

"I lift up my eyes to the mountains–where does my help come from? My help comes from the Lord, the Maker of heaven and earth."

Psalm 121:1-2

We will all need help at some point or another in this journey of life. This is simply part of our human condition. Isn't it wonderful that we can look up, focus on our Creator, and know that help is here?!

~Rev. Chris H.

3 things I am thankful for today:

1.____________________

2.____________________

3.____________________

What is one thing God wants me to do for Him today?

Passing LOVE Forward

Be still for 3 minutes; write down where you would be without God in your life. Thank God for His everlasting love and His loving kindness to you. Think: who can you shower with loving-kindness, even though they humanly may not deserve it?

~Ruth N.

"The Lord appeared to us in the past, saying: "I have loved you with an everlasting love; I have drawn you with unfailing kindness."

Jeremiah 31:3

3 things I am thankful for today:

1.____________________

2.____________________

3.____________________

What is one thing God wants me to do for Him today?

Together

"Those who know your name trust in you, for you, Lord, have never forsaken those who seek you."

Psalm 9:10

I know that God doesn't promise I will never face loss or suffering; but it is so very comforting to know that I won't go it alone. He will never abandon me in times of trouble. I need only to "take it to the Lord in prayer." Thank You, Lord, for being my "Wingman."

~Susan M.

3 things I am thankful for today:

1.____________________

2.____________________

3.____________________

What is one thing God wants me to do for Him today?

Hiding Place

With God at our right hand, we are secure. He does not abandon us; He rescues us because He delights in us. When we cry for help, He hears our voice. When we walk in God's wisdom, He keeps us safe. God is our Rock and our Redeemer. He is our hiding place.

~Chris C.

"Keep me safe, my God, for in you I take refuge."
Psalm 16:1

3 things I am thankful for today:

1.__________

2.__________

3.__________

What is one thing God wants me to do for Him today?

Roped Together

"Though one may be overpowered, two can defend themselves. A cord of three strands is not quickly broken."

Ecclesiastes 4:12

Each strand by itself is strong, but its strength is multiplied greatly when those strands come together to form a rope. Our spiritual rope finds its strength when the strands are braided together with God. I am roped together through a Bible Study here in the Village. Think about who you are "roped" with.

~Peggy H.

3 things I am thankful for today:

1.____________________

2.____________________

3.____________________

What is one thing God wants me to do for Him today?

A Comfort and a Challenge

Reflecting on this verse brings to mind my inherent goodness as one of God's creations. For all my faults, I understand that God made me this way; yet the challenge is to participate, to respond to God with gratitude and efforts to grow in virtue and holiness.

~Paula D.

"Yet you, Lord, are our Father. We are the clay, you are the potter; we are all the work of your hand."

Isaiah 64:8

3 things I am thankful for today:

1.____________________

2.____________________

3.____________________

What is one thing God wants me to do for Him today?

Can't Sleep

"He will not let your foot slip–he who watches over you will not slumber; indeed, he who watches over Israel will neither slumber nor sleep."

Psalm 121:3-4

It is not unusual for many of us to wake up in the middle of the night to find that our minds will not go back to sleep. Isn't it good to know we have a 24/7 God? He is up and ready to listen and share His word with us. Next time you can't sleep, give Him a call.

~Becky M.

3 things I am thankful for today:

1.__________

2.__________

3.__________

What is one thing God wants me to do for Him today?

A Gift So Great

Some things are "hard to imagine," but being unable to even conceive of what's in store? How can we even come close? The Bible says we can have the mind of Christ. By becoming Christ-like in our thoughts and actions, we CAN begin to imagine.

~Diane G.

"...What no eye has seen, what no ear has heard, and what no human mind has conceived"–the things God has prepared for those who love him–"

1 Corinthians 2:9

3 things I am thankful for today:

1.____________

2.____________

3.____________

What is one thing God wants me to do for Him today?

Our Worldly Situation

"I have a message from God in my heart concerning the sinfulness of the wicked: There is no fear of God before their eyes. In their own eyes they flatter themselves too much to detect or hate their sin."

Psalm 36:1-2

As we view all of the hatred and violence in our world today, we are confused. How can God let these things happen? Where have we gone wrong? Many have turned away from God, and we must pray for a return to the love, mercy, and values of the Lord.

~Dotti K.

3 things I am thankful for today:

1.____________________

2.____________________

3.____________________

What is one thing God wants me to do for Him today?

Safety

When mighty storms sweep across the plains to threaten us, I look at the mountains in whose foothills HSV is nestled. Time after time, these ancient Ouachita mountains steer the storms away from our doorsteps. The day after such storms, God reminds us that He can still make rainbows.

~Patty M.

"I lift up my eyes to the mountains–where does my help come from?"

Psalm 121:1

3 things I am thankful for today:

1.__________

2.__________

3.__________

What is one thing God wants me to do for Him today?

Believer or Disciple

"Then said Jesus to those Jews which believed on him, If ye continue in my word, then are ye my disciples indeed;"

John 8:31 (KJV)

John 3:16 tells us "believe on the Lord Jesus Christ, and thou shalt be saved". In John 8:31, Jesus speaks to those who had already believed, telling them if they continue (stay) in God's word, they are His disciples (learner, pupil) indeed. There is a difference in being born again and being a disciple (not to be confused with apostle). May we all be pupils of Jesus by studying and obeying God's word.

~Steve R.

3 things I am thankful for today:

1.________________

2.________________

3.________________

What is one thing God wants me to do for Him today?

Retired, but NOT!

We planned our retirement, but God really planned it ahead of us! Here in the Village, as well as in an economically depressed State, we should, where possible, do charitable works for the betterment of others as well as ourselves. We have the time and the resources. Volunteer!

~LunaGram

"For we are God's handiwork, created in Christ Jesus to do good works, which God prepared in advance for us to do."

Ephesians 2:10

3 things I am thankful for today:

1.__________

2.__________

3.__________

What is one thing God wants me to do for Him today?

Grief is Love with Nowhere to Go

"For with much wisdom comes much sorrow; the more knowledge, the more grief."

Ecclesiastes 1:18

As magical as HSV is, it is one of Heaven's Waiting Rooms. Many of our Villagers have lost loved ones. There is an old Swedish proverb that states "shared joy is double joy, but shared sorrow is halved sorrow." Support groups are numerous here. Grief is just your love with nowhere to go. For now...

~Warren W.

3 things I am thankful for today:

1.____________________

2.____________________

3.____________________

What is one thing God wants me to do for Him today?

Change Your Thinking

You can make your thoughts go the way you want them to go more than you think. Practice thinking in different ways while trusting God. Dismiss sinful negative thoughts as soon as possible. Pray to the Lord and confess to Him while trusting Him to take care of you.

~Donna P.

"If we confess our sins, he is faithful and just and will forgive us our sins and purify us from all unrighteousness."

1 John 1:9

3 things I am thankful for today:

1.______________________________

2.______________________________

3.______________________________

What is one thing God wants me to do for Him today?

Courage

"For the Spirit God gave us does not make us timid, but gives us power, love and self-discipline."

2 Timothy 1:7

I have sometimes found myself in a group where gossipy, unkind words are said, or have encountered a TV show or movie with uncomfortable scenes. Lord, please continually remind me to be strong, using self-control to leave or de-fuse situations in conflict with Your word.

~Chris S.

3 things I am thankful for today:

1.____________________

2.____________________

3.____________________

What is one thing God wants me to do for Him today?

Eliminate Fear and Anxiety

God's gift comes with a command to love one another. When we love in faith, there is no risk, no anxiety, nothing to fear. There is no way to fail when we love. Trusting the promise of God allows us to give ourselves to others freely without fear. It is okay to turn down the volume on the "fear meter."

~Jim H.

"There is no fear in love. But perfect love drives out fear, because fear has to do with punishment. The one who fears is not made perfect in love."

1 John 4:18

3 things I am thankful for today:

1.____________________

2.____________________

3.____________________

What is one thing God wants me to do for Him today?

Serve from Your Saucer

"You prepare a table before me in the presence of my enemies. You anoint my head with oil; my cup overflows."

Psalm 23:5

The Lord supplies us more than we ourselves need. It is our responsibility to use the overflow from our personal cup onto our saucer in service to others for God's glory.

~Jody M.

3 things I am thankful for today:

1.__________

2.__________

3.__________

What is one thing God wants me to do for Him today?

Praying for Others

What a privilege to pray for others. After reading Sometimes He Whispers, Sometimes He Roars by Marilynn Chadwick, I began writing down the names the Lord has given me to pray for: family, church, friends, ministries, missions, projects, and problems. Dividing the list into 7 days makes the list manageable and compelling! This morning, I woke up thinking, "It's Friday! Who all do I get to pray for today?!"

~Sue K.

"...since the day we heard about you, we have not stopped praying for you..."

Colossians 1:9

3 things I am thankful for today:

1.____________________

2.____________________

3.____________________

What is one thing God wants me to do for Him today?

Satan's Unseen Traps

"'Be careful, or your hearts will be weighed down with carousing, drunkenness and the anxieties of life, and that day will close on you suddenly like a trap.'"
Luke 21:34

Right now, take an honest personal inventory. What is dulling your mind or weighing your heart down? Maybe too much wasteful computer or phone time? Maybe worry about tomorrow's "could-happens," or guilt over yesterday's "I-should-haves?" We must be careful for Satan likes his trap of preoccupy-distracting-busyness to keep us from listening to our Lord.

~Ruth N.

3 things I am thankful for today:

1.____________________

2.____________________

3.____________________

What is one thing God wants me to do for Him today?

Needs, Wants, Desires

Our culture today tends to reinforce "it's all about me" "I'm most important." "What do I need, want, desire?" We need to dispel that attitude, for the Bible tells us to put others above ourselves, doing so in love. Though it takes effort, when we do, we know God will take care of our needs, wants, desires.

~Debbie R.

"Be devoted to one another in love. Honor one another above yourselves."

Romans 12:10

3 things I am thankful for today:

1.__________

2.__________

3.__________

What is one thing God wants me to do for Him today?

Let's Go to Work!

"May the favor of the Lord our God rest on us; establish the work of our hands for us–yes, establish the work of our hands."

Psalm 90:17

Flowers can give beauty and joy to others. Rides provide for the real need that many have, and meals can nourish a friend physically as it nourishes you spiritually. Cover your work in prayer today so that it can glorify the One who established it for you.

~Reba L.

3 things I am thankful for today:

1.____________________

2.____________________

3.____________________

What is one thing God wants me to do for Him today?

12. Bloom Where You Are Planted

by Peggy Hadley

Retirement felt like leaving the fast lane of life and hitting a brick wall. Years of a very organized life did not lend itself to doing "nothing," trading the flatlands of Kansas to the richness of the Natural State of Arkansas. Hot Springs Village was definitely not mentioned in my wedding vows.

In fall 2004, Bloom Where You Are Planted was the theme of the very first ladies' NEWcomer class at Mountainside Church. I didn't relate right away. Moving from the sunny open prairielands to a dark forest had left me feeling wilted, perhaps even dying. Shock paralyzed me. Stubbornness kept Kansas in my rear-view mirror constantly. My focus was on all that I left behind.

NewComers taught me that we are like an uprooted plant that was once thriving and, when (what we perceived as) sad changes come our way, we begin to draw back and wither. We need to take great care of ourselves and be carefully transplanted.

Did you know God is GREAT at transplanting people! Without God in our lives, we are like an old plant left unattended. Without His Word, without Scriptures, we wilt. Once we allow ourselves to be transplanted, we begin to bloom again. You gardeners know what I am talking about!

Imagine that the soil surrounding our lives is GOD. He surrounds us with His love, provides support through His people, nourishes us through His Word and, in Him, our roots can grow deep, enabling us to develop into all that HE wants us to be. God is like Miracle Gro.

God also puts Christian people in our lives to nurture us, serve as models for us, encourage us, pray for us, and hold us accountable. We can choose the "soil" in which we will be planted…so choose carefully. Choose the good soil of God, godly people, and things that fill you and nourish your heart and your days. Ephesians 3:17 tells us to be rooted and established in love to know the measure of Christ's love and to know the fullness of God.

Gradually, the greatness that God had laid out for my life came into view. He had obviously been pruning me over time and, my thanks to Him, He never gave up! When I realized, "You can water your woes or fertilize your faith," my attitude became more positive and my heart more thankful.

When we allow God into our lives, homes, and activities, He waters us, refreshes us, prunes off the old useless "things" (the baggage in our lives), and then restores us! Just like transplanted flowers when placed in a new pot with fresh new dirt, beauty happens.

The beauty for me grew into a wonderful church family and a nurturing Bible study group, which has met faithfully every Monday morning for 15 years. My Christian lady friends fertilize my faith, and the service opportunities throughout the Village and outside her gates refresh my soul. Yes, God is like Miracle Gro, and I praise Him for everything.

My prayer is that you have a warm and friendly church family and a Bible study group where you can grow in God's Spirit through the warmth of Christian fellowship. May your heart find how to move forward, whatever your journey, with contentment and the joy that comes from knowing God. Like an open flower, joy can be seen in our eyes, our smile, even the way we walk; it is an outward expression of your inner relationship with God. Grow and bloom wherever God plants you!

> *"Now you are the body of Christ, and each one of you is a part of it."* 1 Corinthians 12:27
>
> *"Let the peace of Christ rule in your hearts, since as members of one body you were called to peace. And be thankful."* Colossians 3:15

Here by Choice

Hot Springs Village embodies this proverb. One can join clubs, boards, associations, teams, or one of 25+ churches and no one checks your bank account to see if you "measure up." What qualifies you is your God-given ability. Most residents are here because they choose to be, not because circumstances force them to be. And...the Lord has made us all!

~Warren W.

"Rich and poor have this in common: The Lord is the Maker of them all."

Proverbs 22:2

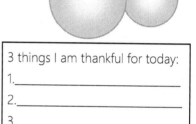

3 things I am thankful for today:

1.____________________

2.____________________

3.____________________

What is one thing God wants me to do for Him today?

Sovereign Magnificence

"The Word became flesh and made his dwelling among us. We have seen his glory, the glory of the one and only Son, who came from the Father, full of grace and truth."

John 1:14

They were expecting a king to sit on a throne! No one expected a baby to make all things new. Plus, Jesus lived an exemplary life, free from all sin. He gave us the perfect example of how to live in line with God's authority. Let us live a life full of grace and truth, as we were taught.

~Vickie H.

3 things I am thankful for today:

1.____________________

2.____________________

3.____________________

What is one thing God wants me to do for Him today?

God in the People We Meet

How much do we celebrate the idea at Christmas that God became incarnate to live with us. How much do I remember, today and every day, that God still is incarnate in me, in His creatures, in the people around me, and especially in the person in front of me at any time?

~Jim H.

"Jesus answered her, 'If you knew the gift of God and who it is that asks you for a drink, you would have asked him and he would have given you living water.'… The woman said, 'I know that Messiah' (called Christ) 'is coming. When he comes, he will explain everything to us.' Then Jesus declared, 'I, the one speaking to you–I am he.'"

John 4:10, 25-26

3 things I am thankful for today:

1.__________

2.__________

3.__________

What is one thing God wants me to do for Him today?

Our Forever Home

"My father's house has many rooms; if that were not so, would I have told you that I am going there to prepare a place for you?"

John 14:2

This passage helpss me believe in our life after death with God in our heavenly home. It helps us not worry about our ultimate death, but know that we will be forever happy in God's presence. We do not expect actual rooms or mansions, but a loving place adoring our God.

~Dotti K.

3 things I am thankful for today:

1.____________________

2.____________________

3.____________________

What is one thing God wants me to do for Him today?

Where to Go with Stress

I love Psalms! This book was written by someone who truly knew about stress, anxiety, pain, and suffering – King David! So, when I'm not able to sleep or I experience a bad day, I find prayers for peace, comfort, joy, and yes, love. Try it. You have nothing to lose and so much to gain. And you don't have to pay a doctor one penny!

~Phillis R.

"When anxiety was great within me, your consolation brought me joy."
Psalm 94:19

3 things I am thankful for today:

1.__________

2.__________

3.__________

What is one thing God wants me to do for Him today?

Extravagant Generosity

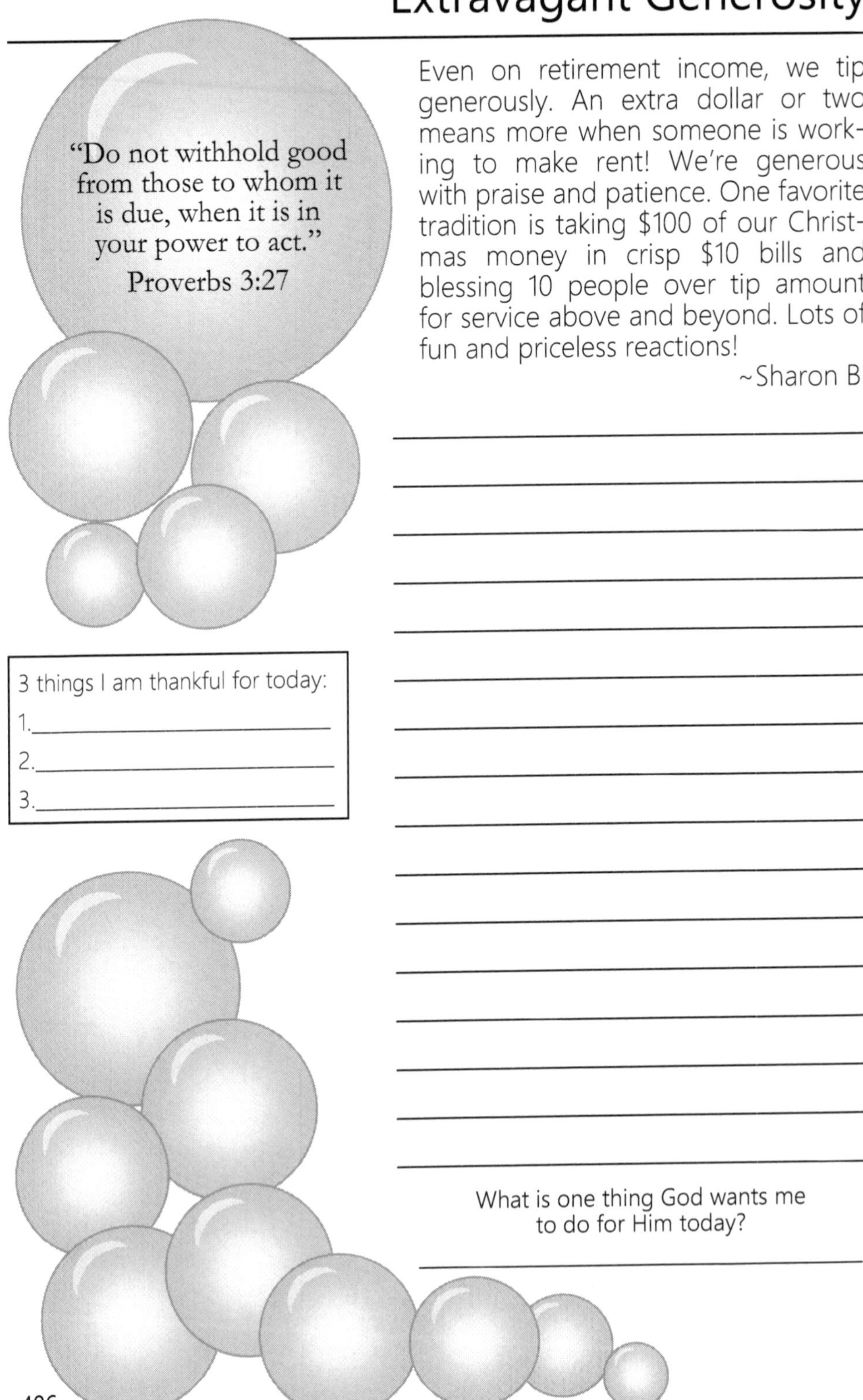

"Do not withhold good from those to whom it is due, when it is in your power to act."
Proverbs 3:27

Even on retirement income, we tip generously. An extra dollar or two means more when someone is working to make rent! We're generous with praise and patience. One favorite tradition is taking $100 of our Christmas money in crisp $10 bills and blessing 10 people over tip amount for service above and beyond. Lots of fun and priceless reactions!

~Sharon B.

3 things I am thankful for today:

1.__________

2.__________

3.__________

What is one thing God wants me to do for Him today?

Look for Him

After Hagar learned that God did indeed see her in her trial, she asked herself if she was looking for Him. She realized, as we should, that looking for God instead of taking the matter into our own hands should be our first resort instead of our last. Too often, we only call on God after all of our attempts have failed.

~Suzan R.

"And she called the name of the Lord that spake unto her, Thou God seest me: for she said, Have I also here looked after him that seeth me?"

Genesis 16:13 (KJV)

3 things I am thankful for today:

1.____________________

2.____________________

3.____________________

What is one thing God wants me to do for Him today?

Hot Springs Village Beauty

"But the land you
are crossing the Jordan
to take possession of is a
land of mountains and valleys
that drinks rain from heaven.
It is a land the Lord your God
cares for; the eyes of the Lord
your God are continually on it
from the beginning of
the year to its end."

Deuteronomy 11:11-12

Do we think of God's beautiful creation here in the Village or do we take it for granted? Many of us moved here to enjoy this forest, and all four seasons; it's nature at its best. In all you see, in all you do, and in all you speak, praise God for His great provisions to us here.

~Peggy H.

3 things I am thankful for today:

1.____________________

2.____________________

3.____________________

What is one thing God wants me to do for Him today?

A Positive Move

My husband was a career service man. We moved 42 times on three different continents. When we retired to the Village in 1983, it became our place of refuge, our place to call "home." God led us to HSV to help build a community that welcomes everyone.

~Patty M.

"For I was hungry and you gave me something to eat, I was thirsty and you gave me something to drink, I was a stranger and you invited me in,"
Matthew 25:35

"My people will live in peaceful dwelling places, in secure homes, in undisturbed places of rest."
Isaiah 32:18

3 things I am thankful for today:

1.__________

2.__________

3.__________

What is one thing God wants me to do for Him today?

New in Town

"Have I not commanded you? Be strong and courageous. Do not be afraid; do not be discouraged, for the Lord your God will be with you wherever you go."
Joshua 1:9

You miss old friends and far-away family; you miss the old neighborhood, where everyone knows your name. You need a new church home, a new hairdresser, a new plumber. You get lost on the winding roads. You can't imagine ever fitting in. Trust in God's plan for you! He's with you every step of the way.

~Susan M.

3 things I am thankful for today:

1.____________________

2.____________________

3.____________________

What is one thing God wants me to do for Him today?

Be Not Afraid

I just love how many times we are told in Scripture "Do not be afraid." The Glory of the Lord shining around the shepherds must have been terrifying. But this is indeed great news for every day of the year. No matter how terrifying our circumstances, our Savior lives!

~Kathy C.

"But the angel said to them, 'Do not be afraid. I bring you good news that will cause great joy for all the people. Today in the town of David a Savior has been born to you; he is the Messiah, the Lord.'"

Luke 2:10-11

3 things I am thankful for today:

1.____________________

2.____________________

3.____________________

What is one thing God wants me to do for Him today?

He Chooses Us

"The Spirit you received does not make you slaves, so that you live in fear again; rather, the Spirit you received brought about your adoption to sonship. And by him we cry, 'Abba, Father.'"

Romans 8:15

Many years ago, a series of unexpected, sudden deaths of friends and relatives took a devastating toll on immediate family. In hindsight, it's uplifting to recognize that our heavenly Father adopted and sheltered us. He guided a young widow with 3 children who cried out to Him, freeing us from the slavery of despair.

~Chris S.

3 things I am thankful for today:

1.__________

2.__________

3.__________

What is one thing God wants me to do for Him today?

Beauty in the Desert

Imagine our souls are a flower. As we allow God to guide our thoughts, emotions, and actions, filling us with Himself, our faith begins to blossom. Our Faith then brings beauty and sweet fragrance to those around us, even while living in and through a desert season in our life."

~Ruth N.

"The Lord will guide you always; he will satisfy your needs in a sun-scorched land and will strengthen your frame. You will be like a well-watered garden, like a spring whose waters never fail."

Isaiah 58:11

3 things I am thankful for today:

1.__________

2.__________

3.__________

What is one thing God wants me to do for Him today?

Wholehearted Devotion

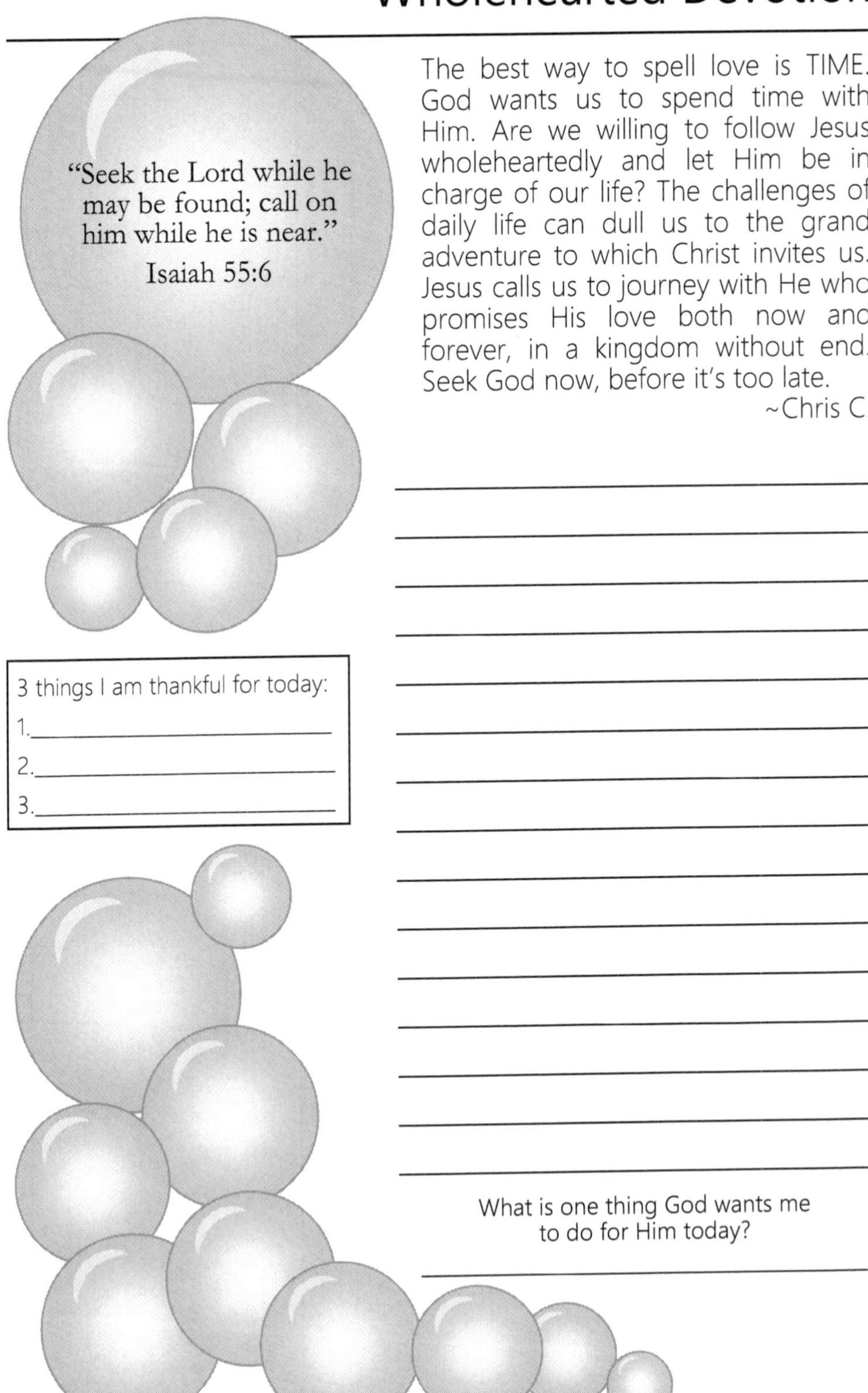

"Seek the Lord while he may be found; call on him while he is near."
Isaiah 55:6

The best way to spell love is TIME. God wants us to spend time with Him. Are we willing to follow Jesus wholeheartedly and let Him be in charge of our life? The challenges of daily life can dull us to the grand adventure to which Christ invites us. Jesus calls us to journey with He who promises His love both now and forever, in a kingdom without end. Seek God now, before it's too late.

~Chris C.

3 things I am thankful for today:

1.____________________

2.____________________

3.____________________

What is one thing God wants me to do for Him today?

The Church Nursery

A cross-stitched version of this verse was framed and hung in a prominent spot in our church nursery. It brought many a smile to the faces of parents and volunteer nursery workers – and lodged in our hearts! The Resurrection is one of the great mysteries of the New Testament, and this verse forecasts such hope for believers!

~Sue K.

"Listen, I tell you a mystery: We will not all sleep, but we will all be changed–"

1 Corinthians 15:51

3 things I am thankful for today:

1.________________

2.________________

3.________________

What is one thing God wants me to do for Him today?

A Very Special Friend

"I no longer call you servants, because a servant does not know his master's business. Instead, I have called you friends, for everything that I learned from my Father I have made known to you."

John 15:15

Do you have a special friend... someone who knows you deeply, who listens and counsels in love, who cares about you in a unique way? Jesus, the Son of God, calls us friends. How awesome!! We can talk to Him, telling Him anything and everything. He listens. He counsels in love. He is love and He calls us friends.

~Debbie R.

3 things I am thankful for today:

1.__________________

2.__________________

3.__________________

What is one thing God wants me to do for Him today?

Take a Stand!

We know that Jesus showed kindness and compassion and that He expects us to do the same. Sometimes that means taking a stand against injustice! Our God is a God of justice and mercy. When the poor or needy are ignored and their rights trampled, our God expects His followers to have the courage to defend those rights!

~Vickie H.

"Speak up and judge fairly; defend the rights of the poor and needy."

Proverbs 31:9

3 things I am thankful for today:

1.____________________

2.____________________

3.____________________

What is one thing God wants me to do for Him today?

Get Covered

"He will cover you with his feathers, and under his wings you will find refuge; his faithfulness will be your shield and rampart."
Psalm 91:4

The habit of journaling prayers has given me the opportunity to look back to see how, if, or when God answered those prayers. His faithfulness to answer some specific, tiny detail again and again has given me complete confidence that His "feathers" provide the greatest shield for my life. Won't you be covered today?

~Reba L.

3 things I am thankful for today:

1.____________________

2.____________________

3.____________________

What is one thing God wants me to do for Him today?

Confession

Here is a wonderful promise: if we confess our sins, God will forgive us! So, don't wait – confess today. Don't carry around your burdens of guilt and shame. Confess and be made clean!

~Julie K

"If we confess our sins, he is faithful and just and will forgive us our sins and purify us from all unrighteousness."

1 John 1:9

3 things I am thankful for today:

1.____________________

2.____________________

3.____________________

What is one thing God wants me to do for Him today?

A New Mindset

"Then he said to them, 'Watch out! Be on your guard against all kinds of greed; life does not consist in an abundance of possessions.'"
Luke 12:15

Moving from a big-city corporate environment to the Village, I found that status and materialism are not priorities. For example, a retired brain surgeon could be playing in your Pickleball match, but everyone in the game is only there to have fun and play the best Pickleball they can play. It's a totally different mindset.

~Vickie H.

3 things I am thankful for today:

1.________________________

2.________________________

3.________________________

What is one thing God wants me to do for Him today?

I Belong to Him

Always be joyful. Always keep on praying. No matter what happens, always be thankful, for this is God's will for you because you belong to Jesus Christ.

~Linda N.

"...encourage the disheartened, help the weak, be patient with everyone. Make sure that nobody pays back wrong for wrong, but always strive to do what is good for each other and for everyone else..."

Thessalonians 5:14-17

3 things I am thankful for today:

1.________________________

2.________________________

3.________________________

What is one thing God wants me to do for Him today?

Change

"Listen, I tell you a mystery: We will not all sleep, but we will all be changed–"

1 Corinthians 15:51

Change can be difficult, but sometimes, in order to survive, we have to start a change process. We sometimes need to get rid of old memories, habits, and past traditions. Only when freed from past burdens can we take advantage of the present and be prepared to enjoy the beautiful future that awaits us.

~Steve B.

3 things I am thankful for today:

1.____________________

2.____________________

3.____________________

What is one thing God wants me to do for Him today?

Hover Over Me, God!

Sometimes, we're not sure what's next for us. Life may seem dark; our future may seem empty, but God never stops working! Ask Him to hover over your life, to do something, to make something of the rest of your days! Our beautiful, creative God can make something wonderful of each season of our lives!

~Marilyn C.

"Now the earth was formless and empty, darkness was over the surface of the deep, and the Spirit of God was hovering over the waters."

Genesis 1:2

3 things I am thankful for today:

1.________________

2.________________

3.________________

What is one thing God wants me to do for Him today?

Build a Ship Where?

"By faith Noah, when warned about things not yet seen, in holy fear built an ark to save his family…"

Hebrews 11:7

What faith! To build an ark on dry land – and not a cloud in the sky! What further faith – Noah preached for 120 years without a single convert, yet he never gave up. Ridicule and scorn pelted down like rain, yet he persevered. His faith was honored by God, and it saved his entire family and all species of the earth from destruction.

~Diane G.

3 things I am thankful for today:

1.____________________

2.____________________

3.____________________

What is one thing God wants me to do for Him today?

Taking Time for God

How blessed we are when we spend time with our children! God feels the same way. Bask in the sweetness of your loving Father. Send up tiny bubble prayers all day long. It is right to thank Him, praise Him, and share our needs and wants. He is the author of JOY. Tell Him know how you love and appreciate Him.

~Phillis R.

"Surely you have granted him unending blessings and made him glad with the joy of your presence."

Psalm 21:6

3 things I am thankful for today:

1.__________

2.__________

3.__________

What is one thing God wants me to do for Him today?

Growing Old Gracefully

"But blessed is the one who trusts in the Lord, whose confidence is in him. They will be like a tree planted by the water that sends out its roots by the stream. It does not fear when heat comes; its leaves are always green. It has no worries in a year of drought and never fails to bear fruit."
Jeremiah 17: 7-8

With each passing year, like it or not, our physical bodies deteriorate a little, but not so with our soul. The person who trusts in the Lord, who spends time in sweet fellowship of speaking, listening, and being still together, will flourish even when the body has no strength to go on.

~Ruth N.

3 things I am thankful for today:

1.____________________________

2.____________________________

3.____________________________

What is one thing God wants me to do for Him today?

Contentment

Contentment will not dwell with anyone who has hatred, jealousy, or envy in their heart. Life is too short to grumble over misfortune. If we cannot change the circumstances in which we must live, we can learn to overcome them. Contentment is not a gift; it is an achievement.

~Patty M.

"...for I have learned, in whatsoever state I am, therewith to be content."
Philippians 4:11 (KJV)

3 things I am thankful for today:

1.________________________

2.________________________

3.________________________

What is one thing God wants me to do for Him today?

Understanding

"The Lord looks down from heaven on all mankind to see if there are any who understand, any who seek God."

Psalm 14:2

People will look at your past and judge you from there, God will look at your future. Satan always puts us down, God always encourages and lifts us up. Life can be hard, but nurturing a relationship with God doesn't have to be.

~Peggy H.

3 things I am thankful for today:

1.____________________

2.____________________

3.____________________

What is one thing God wants me to do for Him today?

Renewing Me Day by Day

Moving from a youth-driven community to the Village gave me new perspective on aging. People from all over are re-inventing themselves here, with newly freed time and loads of options. I felt God healing my burnt-out self, day by day, at church, at the gym, with new friends. I no longer feel my life is nearly over. God can use my renewed self in this Village.

~Sharon B.

"Therefore we do not lose heart. Though outwardly we are wasting away, yet inwardly we are being renewed day by day."

2 Corinthians 4:16

3 things I am thankful for today:

1.__________

2.__________

3.__________

What is one thing God wants me to do for Him today?

God's Love Envelops Us

"How priceless is your unfailing love, O God! People take refuge in the shadow of your wings."

Psalm 36:7

When problems develop, how can we survive without taking refuge in God's love and protection? People who do not believe that must suffer immensely all alone. When you face illness, family problems, job problems, do you turn to God for help and healing?

~Dotti K.

3 things I am thankful for today:

1.____________________

2.____________________

3.____________________

What is one thing God wants me to do for Him today?

Being in a Family

God doesn't promise better weather and fairer days to His followers... because even those who don't follow Him are still His creatures and He loves them because of that. He does promise that loving all His creatures, regardless of their response, makes us "family." And that's enough.

~Jim H.

"But I tell you, love your enemies and pray for those who persecute you, that you may be children of your Father in heaven. He causes his sun to rise on the evil and the good, and sends rain on the righteous and the unrighteous."

Matthew 5:44-45

3 things I am thankful for today:

1.____________________

2.____________________

3.____________________

What is one thing God wants me to do for Him today?

Afterward

When Village residents are gathered, within a matter of minutes, they begin to share stories about their grandchildren. Here are just a few of the cute little God-related quotes that our children and grandchildren are known for.

4-year-old Max saw the
Easter cross stating,
"He is Risen!"
in our front yard and
asked what it meant.
I said, "Even though Jesus
died, He is now risen and
in heaven with God."
Max said, "I'm going to tell
people about that!" and
went door-to-door
telling the neighbors!

Watching a beautiful sunrise,
2-year-old Stella asked,
"Grandma Vickie,
did you do that?"
I responded,
"No Stella, God did that!"
She looked puzzled and said,
"I've never met Him!"
I smiled and said,
"You will."

When granddaughter Barbra
was barely talking, we kept
her Christmas Eve. We told
the Christmas story
over and over Once more,
before bedtime, we asked,
"Now, Barbra, whose
birthday is it tomorrow?"
She thought, then exclaimed,
"Chucky Jesus!"

Watching the Disney
version of Moses, my
6-year-old grandson asked:"
Nana, why was God so
mean to those people?"
I replied that they had made
Him angry. He immediately
stood up, pushed his pizza
away, put his little hands
on his hips, and said,
"Well, remind me never to
make God mad, I don't like
those plague things."

When our son was
4 years old, my husband
was digging a hole to
plant a shrub in the yard.
Our son inquired if they
were going to see
God's hands. My husband,
perplexed, asked what he was
talking about, and he answered,
"We sing that song that says
'He has the whole
world in His hands!'"

Our Christmas custom
was to bake a sheet cake,
cut it in half and let our
granddaughters decorate the
cake with icing saying
"Happy Birthday Jesus!"
After nap time, we had a
birthday party. The 4-year-old
surprised me by saying,
"Can we wait a little longer,
I really think He might show up!"

Our little granddaughter,
Lilly, was finger painting
with me recently.
The sun shone into the
kitchen, casting a reflection
of a cross onto the ceiling.
Lilly excitedly exclaimed;
"Look Grandma, Jesus is here!"
Yes, indeed. Jesus is here.

A friend took her young
grandson to a Christmas
Eve service. When it came
time for communion, she was
whispering things to help
him understand. So, as she
discussed the body and
blood and Christ's death, in
alarm, he shouted out in
the quiet sanctuary,
"Baby Jesus died?!?"

As we studied the Fruit
of the Spirit in Sunday
School, the children
wanted to add a fruit:
Courage.
This was a huge word
to them...to take
courage over someone
or something.

On a hot summer day,
in a car with no air
conditioner, we pulled up
beside another car at a
stop light. My 2-year old
looked at the long-haired
young man in the next car,
then waved and yelled,
"Hi Jesus!" I asked him why
he called him Jesus. He said,
"Because he is! I saw him last
week at the grocery store too."
I was happy when the
red light turned green.

Today, out of the blue,
my 7 year old grandson
said he would do anything
for Jesus. I asked him why
and he said,
"Because He never did
anything wrong."
What trust he has in Jesus!

Our 2-year old had problems falling asleep. His mom decided she'd try to "pray about it." She began their prayer with, "Lord, we know Wade has trouble falling asleep. Tonight, we ask that the minute his head hits the pillow, he will be fast asleep." The toddler threw himself back on his pillow, then sat straight back up and said, "Try it again!"

The little girl asked her daddy, "If Jesus is up in heaven, why do we look down when we pray?"

Our young grandson was visiting church with us. As we greeted the other parishioners, saying "God bless you!", he looked confused. He said, "I thought you only say that when someone sneezes!"

When my third grader arrived home from his first day at a new school, I asked him if he learned anything? I'd heard the first day would be mostly rules and expectations. He said, "Well, they didn't talk much about Jesus, but they sure want us to act like Him."

The young boy asked his mom, "Do you really think Jesus will forgive us for lying about Santa Claus?"

Two brothers were discussing how the younger loved protein bars and always wanted one the minute he got home from daycare. The older brother asked, "What do you love most, protein bars or Jesus?" Without hesitation, the younger replied, "Bars!" His brother said, "Uh oh, you won't get to heaven!"

Our children's lesson was about the Garden of Eden. The children heard that death occurred when Adam and Eve ate from the "Bad Tree." One little 4 year old boy raised his hand and said, "My Grandfather ate from that bad tree." When the teachers asked why he had said that, the boy said very seriously, "Because he died."

"And he said: 'Truly I tell you, unless you change and become like little children, you will never enter the kingdom of heaven.'" Matthew 18:3

"But Jesus called the children to him and said, 'Let the little children come to me, and do not hinder them, for the kingdom of God belongs to such as these. Truly I tell you, anyone who will not receive the kingdom of God like a little child will never enter it.'" Luke 18:16-17

Contributing Authors

1. Alice Hill
   jialhill32@yahoo.com
2. Becky Mueller
   rbmuel64@gmail.com
3. Bess Moore
4. Betty Wilhite
   bettywhilhite@gmail.com
5. Chris C.
6. Chris Stein
   cks811@suddenlink.net
7. Debbie Carroll
   d2onmaui@hotmail.com
8. Debbie Reed
   debrar1980@gmail.com
9. Debi Scherer
   debischerer@mac.com
10. Diane Gower
    dsgower@gmail.com
11. Donna Parker
    redhead_37075@yahoo.com
12. Dotti Kessen
    Kessendotti@gmail.com

13. Fr. Bill Elser
frbillelser@gmail.com
14. Ike Eisenhauer
ike.eisenhauer.hoho.@statefarm.com
15. Jan Folstad
janfolstad@sbcglobal.net
16. Jim Hengstenberg
jhengstenberg@hotmail.com
17. JoNancy Sundberg
hsvcatmom@sbcglobal.net
18. Jody Moore
pupemom42@bellsouth.net
19. Julie Keck
juliekeck@aol.com
20. Kathy Clark
kathy@begintodayorganizing.com
21. Kathy Sanders
kathysandersart@sbcglobal.net
22. Linda Norman
lnorman4@aol.com
23. Lindsey Ray
lindsey@elrodfirm.com
24. LunaGram
tujour@icloud.com
25. Lynda Grasse
lynda.grasse@gmail.com

26. Marilyn Carstens
    mcarstens6pinlane@gmail.com
27. Marty Schnoebelen
    marty.schnoebelen@gmail.com
28. Nancy Matthew
    nancymatthew40@gmail.com
29. Patty Vineyard MacDonald
    mac.pat4321@gmail.com
30. Paula Doyle
    pauladoyle70@gmail.com
31. Peggy Hadley
    hadleyinhsv@sbcglobal.net
32. Phillis Ruggieri
    prsinger@att.net
33. Reba Lee
    deanlee6377@gmail.com
34. Rev. Chris Hemund
    revhemund@gmail.com
35. Rosemary Farrell
    rosefarrell@hotmail.com
36. Ruth Neal
    ruthneal@aol.com
37. Sharon Bush
    bushsharonl@yahoo.com
38. Steve Bush
    revstevebush@yahoo.com

39. Steve Rust
sdrust51@gmail.com
40. Steve Wilhite
rodneyswilhite@gmail.com
41. Sue Kilfoy
2jaynsue@gmail.com
42. Sue Maser
skmaser@yahoo.com
43. Susan Viles
suviles@gmail.com
44. Suzan Rust
sqrust@gmail.com
45. Tanya Jones
tjon5555@gmail.com
46. Teela Young
teelacolorado@yahoo.com
47. Vicki Fritz
rvfritz1@sbcglobal.net
48. Vickie Henry
vickiehenry7@gmail.com
49. Warren Walters
w3onseven2012@gmail.com

Acknowledgements

Once again, Suzanne Sadler partnered with me on this, our third *Prayer Bubbles* adventure. Our association began in 1993, when Suzanne joined my company, Feedback Plus. A recent graduate of the University of Texas at Arlington, she impressed all of us with her creativity and organizational skills. She eagerly and efficiently completed whatever project she was asked to do. After she moved on to expand her career at larger companies in the Dallas area, we had little contact with one another over the next 20 years.

Then, early one morning, while sitting on the balcony of the Grand Mayan in Los Cabos, Mexico, surrounded by the first draft of my first faith-based book, *Prayer Bubbles,* I threw my arms up to God, saying "Help!" The content was nearly complete, but the organization was far from anything workable. Suddenly, the name *Suzanne* came to me in God's sweet whisper. On my return to Dallas, and after a quick search on Facebook, we reconnected. She was freelancing! (Don't you just love how God works?) The rest is history. We both worked diligently, compiling all the necessary components for *Prayer Bubbles* and *Prayer Bubbles Daily Journal.* These books have been a blessing to so many; probably me most of all. Suzanne laid out each book, tackled the lion's share of organization and editing, then set everything up on Kindle for publication. She is truly my partner, and I appreciate her so much.

Nancy Smith instantly answered my plea for help to develop the table of contents for this book. The stories were complete, the scriptures and the narratives were submitted, and ALL were scattered around my desk. After a few hours of brainstorming, the structure of the book came together in an orderly fashion.

Ruth Neal and Warren Walters were my spiritual support throughout the making of this book. Each wrote their 10-verse contribution immediately and, when my deadline panic began, they prayed and wrote more verses. They kept me grounded, reminding me that God is in control. This is His book and He will provide. And He always has.

49 additional authors and contributors provided consistent prayer covering throughout the writing of this book. I am forever grateful for their support.

Lastly, I thank my husband, Reb Henry, Nancy Smith, Sue Kilfoy, and Teela Young for help with proofing and editing, such an important part of any book.

About the Author

Vickie Henry grew up in Iola, Kansas. After brief period in New Mexico, she made her home in Dallas, Texas.

Vickie was a banker before owning her market research company, Feedback Plus, Inc., which specialized mystery shopping. An article in the *Wall Street Journal* labeled Vickie as "America's Mystery Shopper." As her business grew, Vickie spent years speaking about customer service, presenting her popular keynote, Would You Do Business with You? to audiences throughout the world.

After selling her company five years ago, Vickie and her husband, Reb, retired in Hot Springs Village, Arkansas. They have two children, seven grandchildren, and one great grandchild. She enjoys golf, Pickleball, table tennis, kayaking, hiking, Bible studies, and her book club. She also volunteers for South Central Arkansas Transit (SCAT), scheduling rides for residents of HSV.

Life is good.

A Note from Vickie

Dear Readers,

Compiling this journal has been a tremendous blessing. I emphasize compiling, though the credit of authorship belongs to me. From the first "nudge," I feel that God has guided every step and every word.

Recently, during prayer time, certain people would enter my mind. I invited a core group of 14 friends to my home for coffee one morning or popcorn that same evening. Most had a copy of my Prayer Bubbles Journal; all are faithful servants of the Lord. Some enjoyed writing and journaling. Most were supportive of a new VILLAGE journal. They said they would pray for me, but a few weren't certain about what they could really contribute – they were not "writers." Then, we recalled 2 Corinthians 12:9: "But he said to me, 'My grace is sufficient for you, for my power is made perfect in weakness.' Therefore, I will boast all the more gladly about my weaknesses, so that Christ's power may rest on me."

That very afternoon, one of my morning coffee friends, who said she was definitely not a writer, sent me 10 scriptures and beautiful commentaries on each one. Once again, it's amazing to watch God at work.

Through the process, my typical sense of urgency was at play. The first few weeks were so exciting! Verses arrived 10-20-30 per day. Soon, 160 verses were ready for the journal pages. Joy filled my heart...until I realized we had 206 to go! Panic set in and, for a moment, I became discouraged (we all know that these emotions are not from God). By the deadline, I had received 483 verses! My mother's favorite reprimand to me, "Honey, where's your faith?" echoed in my mind.

We have a total of 49 contributing authors. My prayer is that each contributor will feel as blessed by it as I do. And the blessings will be continue for years to come. Each morning, as we spend time with God, we will read His Word and a small message, and feel a sense of endearment as we whisper, "Lord, these are words from one of my neighbors! She's my friend. She lives right here in Hot Springs Village with me!" Hopefully, the journals will find their way outside of HSV – there are no boundaries to God's love! You don't have to live in the Village to commune closely with God…but it doesn't hurt! Ha!

I covet your prayers and your feedback!

Vickie Henry
Vickiehenry7@gmail.com
972.743.1750
www.GodsSacredBubble.com

Made in the USA
Lexington, KY
16 November 2019

57159577R00245